Instructor's Media Guide

PSYCHOLOGY

THIRD EDITION

Media & Research Update

Stephen Davis

Joseph J. Palladino

PRENTICE HALL, Upper Saddle River, NJ 07458

10 9 8 7 6 5 4

ISBN 0-13-096811-0

TRADEMARK INFORMATION:
America Online is a registered trademark of America Online, Inc.;
CompuServe is a registered trademark of CompuServe, Incorporated;
Microsoft Windows is a trademark of Microsoft Corporation;
Mosaic is copyrighted by the Board of Trustees of the University of Illinois (UI);
Netscape Navigator is a registered trademark of Netscape Communications Corporation;
JavaScript is a registered trademark of Sun Microsystems;
Internet Explorer is a registered trademark of Microsoft Corporation.

Contents

Preface

This *Media User's Guide* is provided to help you navigate your way through the media resources that accompany ***Psychology, Third Edition: Media and Research Update***, by Stephen F. Davis and Joseph J. Palladino.

Organization of This Guide

This guide is divided into three parts:

- ***Part One*** describes **The Companion Website** and provides navigation tools for using this valuable study aid.

- ***Part Two*** describes the content of **The Psychology Place**, which is available on a subscription basis only. The Activation ID and Password for your free six-month subscription can be found on the inside back cover of your text.

- ***Part Three*** presents an overview of the **"Video Classics in Psychology" CD-ROM** that is packaged free with every copy of the Media & Research Update. In this section you'll find a list of the videos that appear on the CD-Rom, an introduction to each video, and several questions and suggested answers for each video segment.

Logging On

First-time users may log on to the *Companion Webstite* through the following URL: http://www.prenhall.com/davis

Once you access this site, you should choose the Third Edition of Steve Davis and Joseph Palladino's ***Psychology***.

After you click on the Third Edition, you'll have a choice of entering the free **Companion Website** area or the subscription-based **Psychology Place** area. If you choose **The Companion Website**, you'll have an opportunity to customize the site by creating a profile for yourself (see Part One). If you choose **The Psychology Place**, you'll be asked to enter the Activation ID and Password that appear on the inside back cover of the text. As part of your initial log-in, you'll have the opportunity to create your own Password. It is recommended that you write your Activation ID and Password down and keep it in a secure place.

Introductory Psychology is a richly rewarding course that you will most likely remember for the rest of your life. Enjoy!

A Unique Online Study Resource

The Companion Website™

A Unique Online Study Resource
The Companion Website™

As an instructor, you are no doubt familiar with the various supplements produced in conjunction with your textbooks. From videotapes to workbooks, these tools are designed to reinforce the core concepts presented by textbook authors. In addition to traditional print study guides, Prentice Hall now offers online study guides called Companion Websites. To date, over 1,000,000 students have visited Prentice Hall's text-specific Companion Websites.

Prentice Hall Companion Websites allow students to:

- identify key topics in your course.
- take interactive quizzes.
- receive immediate feedback on your answers.
- send your results to instructors via e-mail.
- search the Internet using links that have been selected by field experts.

Companion Websites are easy to use. Their standardized design leads students carefully from one activity to the next, chapter by chapter. Online study guides not only give them a better understanding of the core concepts presented in their textbooks, but they also focus students attention on the most important material in every chapter. Most of all, Companion Websites help students use their study time more effectively.

Section 1
Locating Companion Websites

Not sure if your book has a Companion Website? Visiting the Prentice Hall Companion Website Gallery is the simplest way to find out. Go to the Prentice Hall website at **http://www.prenhall.com** and click on *Companion Website Gallery* in the upper right-hand corner of the screen. Then, in the empty box on the black navigation bar, enter the last name of your textbook's author. To generate a list of Websites that meet your criteria, click on the *Search* button. For example, a search for "Davis" would yield the screen shown in Figure 1. Select the appropriate book by looking at the covers, hyperlinked titles, and brief descriptions.

Notice that some sites are labeled "demo." As such sites are currently under development, you can access only one or two chapters of sample content. Check back frequently since Prentice Hall is constantly adding new titles to the Companion Website Gallery.

Another way to see whether a particular book has a Companion Website is to type the following URL into your Location Toolbar: **http://www.prenhall.com/(lead author)**. The text in parenthesis should be replaced with the name of the lead author of your Prentice Hall textbook. For example, the address for *Psychology* by Stephen F. Davis and Joseph J. Palladino is **http://www.prenhall.com/davis**.

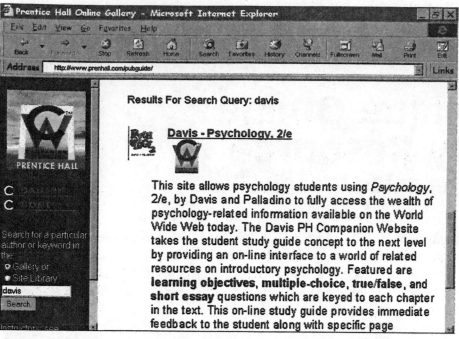

Figure 1. Entering an author's name and clicking on the *Search* button will generate a list of Websites that meet your criteria.

Section 2
Getting Started

On the first page of every Humanities and Social Sciences Companion Website you will find two frames (Figure 2):

Left frame: Navigation Bar

- Syllabus Manager™
- Carol Carter's Student Success Web Supersite
- Your Profile
- Help

Right frame: Content Window

- Link to Web Catalog
- Website Features
- Chapter Menu
- Begin Button

This section will walk you through each of these components.

Navigation Bar

Syllabus Manager

Every Companion Website integrates Syllabus Manager, an online syllabus creation and management utility. After an instructor has created a syllabus using Syllabus Manager, students may enter the syllabus for their course section from any point in the Companion Website. In the Student Login Window (Figure 3), students have the option of searching by *Instructor's Last Name*, *Instructor's E-Mail Address*, or *School Name*.

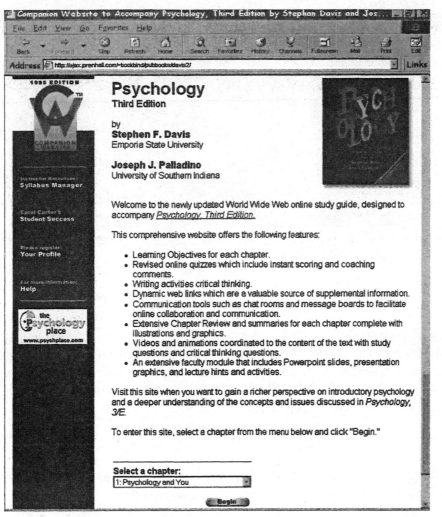

Figure 2. The first page of every Companion Website is divided into two frames: the navigation bar and the content window.

After choosing the button next to the instructor's name, click on the *Search Now* button at the bottom of the screen.

Note that as instructor, you can create different syllabi for each section you teach; be sure to check the section column (Figure 4) before you click on *Open Syllabus*. If you password-protect the syllabus,

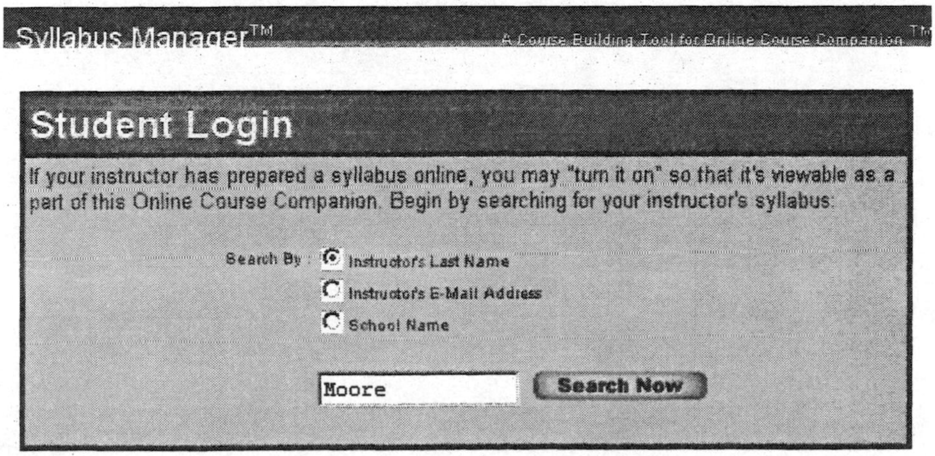

Syllabus Manager™   A Course Building Tool for Online Course Companion ™

Student Login

If your instructor has prepared a syllabus online, you may "turn it on" so that it's viewable as a part of this Online Course Companion. Begin by searching for your instructor's syllabus:

Search By: ⊙ Instructor's Last Name
     ○ Instructor's E-Mail Address
     ○ School Name

Moore   **Search Now**

Figure 3. Students can use the Student Login Window to see whether their instructor has created an online syllabus for the course.

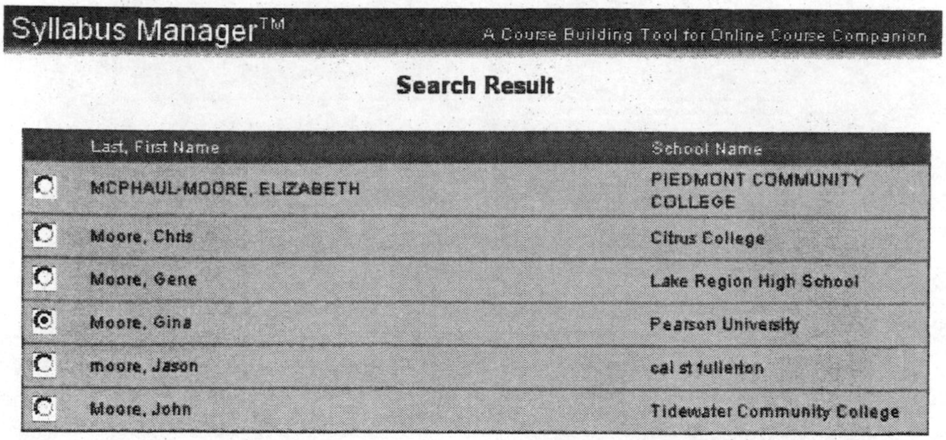

Figure 4. When the search engine generates a list of several syllabi, make sure your students select the syllabus for your section.

students will need to enter the correct password in the Logon screen (Figure 5) before they can continue. Lost passwords can be requested by using the form at the bottom of the screen.

After students gain access to the correct syllabus, course summary information appears in the right frame and a calendar appears in the left frame of the Companion Website (Figure 6). Class dates are highlighted in white, and assignment due dates appear in blue. Clicking on a blue date reveals the assignment for that particular day. To save time, the Companion Website activities for each assignment are linked directly from the syllabus to actual content modules.

Use the following directions to print your syllabus:

- Select the syllabus frame by clicking anywhere on the white background of the syllabus.
- Select *File* from top menu bar and then select *Print Frame* . . .
- Make proper printer settings and click *OK*.

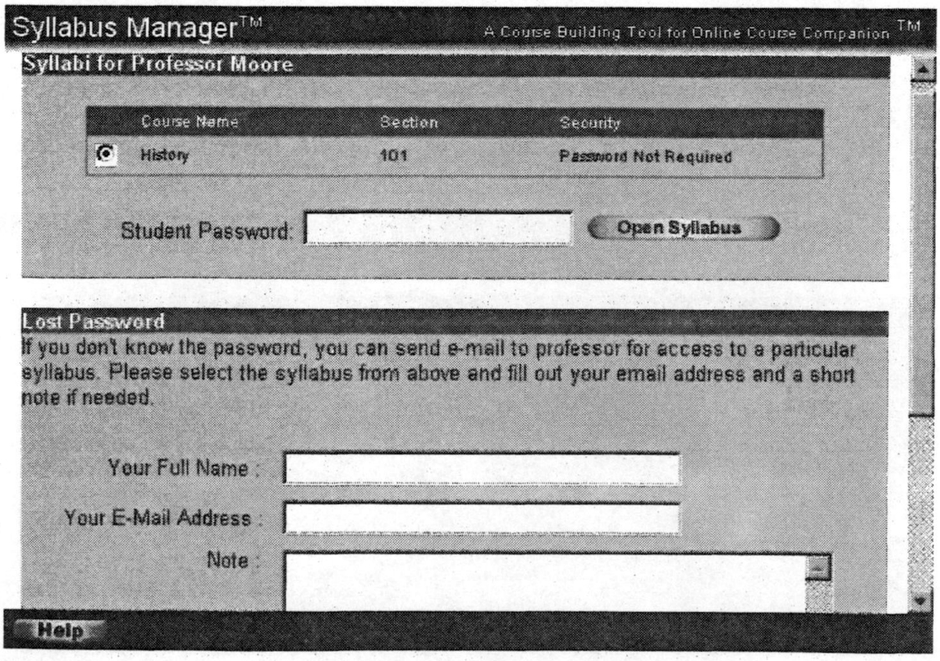

Figure 5. Students should fill out the login screen to enter your syllabus.

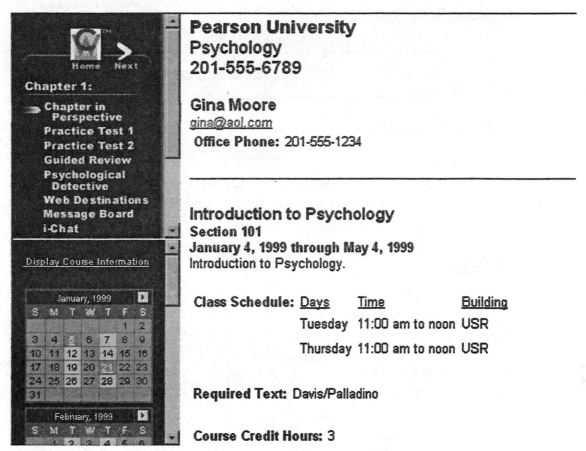

Pearson University
Psychology
201-555-6789

Gina Moore
gina@aol.com
Office Phone: 201-555-1234

Introduction to Psychology
Section 101
January 4, 1999 through May 4, 1999
Introduction to Psychology.

Class Schedule:	Days	Time	Building
	Tuesday	11:00 am to noon	USR
	Thursday	11:00 am to noon	USR

Required Text: Davis/Palladino

Course Credit Hours: 3

Figure 6. Click on a blue assignment due date on the calendar in the left frame to view the homework for that particular class.

Carol Carter's Student Success Web Supersite

Geared towards high school graduates, college students, returning students, and career changers, this resource site is designed to help students select the appropriate path to meet their educational needs. Features include:

- exploration of different majors.
- answers to study skill questions.
- advice from career counselors.
- brief biographies designed to inspire lifelong learners.
- Web links to interesting sites related to student success.

Your Profile

As mentioned in the overview, Companion Websites not only allow students to take interactive quizzes, but they also provide the opportunity to send results to an instructor via e-mail. The *Profile* feature lets students standardize the submission of quiz results. By (carefully) entering their personal information in Figure 7, they can avoid retyping it every time they need to submit homework. Once saved, the information will appear automatically whenever it's required. Students must remember to click on the *E-mail Results* button in the *Results Reporter* each time they want to send data to their instructor.

Students may return to this screen to modify their profile at any time by clicking the *Profile* button located on the navigation bar throughout the site.

After entering their personal data, students should remember to check all of the appropriate boxes under "Send my quiz results to" (Figure 8). If the instuctor prefers to receive results in the body of

Personal Information

	First	Last
My Name:		
E-mail:		

Instructor Information

	Name	E-Mail
Instructor:		
TA:		
Other:		

Figure 7. This form gives you the opportunity to send your results to an instructor via e-mail. By carefully entering your personal information, you can avoid retyping it every time you need to submit homework.

Send my quiz results to:

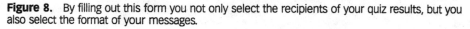

☐	Myself:	As plain text ▾
☐	Instructor:	As plain text ▾
☐	TA:	As plain text ▾
☐	Other:	As plain text ▾

Figure 8. By filling out this form you not only select the recipients of your quiz results, but you also select the format of your messages.

an e-mail message, select either "as plain text" or "as HTML" (for *Navigator* or *Internet Explorer* e-mail). On the other hand, if instructors prefer to receive results as an attachment, select either "as text attachment" or "as HTML attachment" (for *Navigator* or *Internet Explorer* e-mail). Please note that students should always e-mail themselves a copy of your results because Prentice Hall will not save a backup copy.

Due to the volume of submissions, Companion Website e-mail is batched and sent out at thirty minute intervals. Depending on when results are sent to our server for distribution, it may take up to thirty minutes for results to arrive in your professor's inbox. Students should keep this in mind when submitting homework assignments.

In the *Profile* area, students can also subscribe to the site mailing list by entering their name and e-mail address. Companion Website mailing lists alert users of site updates, i-Chat events, and other items directly related to the textbook or website. Prentice Hall does not use mailing lists for marketing or "spam" e-mail purposes.

Help

This brief overview of Companion Website technology addresses questions that other users have had in the past. Topics are organized by module type in the left-hand navigation bar. To learn more about a particular feature, simply click on its name.

Content Window

In addition to a list of website features, the content window on the first page of every Companion Website contains a link to the Web Catalog. Visit the Web Catalog to read a summary of the textbook and view a complete table of contents. To enter the site, (1) select a chapter from the pull-down menu at the bottom of the screen and (2) click *Begin* (Figure 9).

Figure 9. To enter a Companion Website, select a chapter from the pull-down menu at the bottom of the screen and click *Begin*.

Section 3
Navigation

In order to move through a Companion Website effectively, you should use the navigation bar in the left frame of the browser window. The top of the navigation bar (Figure 10) offers controls for moving to the previous chapter, the next chapter, or to the top of the site (the index page).

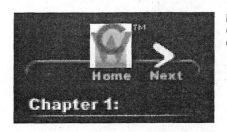

Figure 10. The top of the navigation bar offers controls for moving to the previous chapter, the next chapter, or to the top of the site (the index page).

The middle of the navigation bar (Figure 11) provides links directly to the quiz, research, and communication modules discussed later in this document. Sometimes this area will also include links to individual modules that have been gathered into groups.

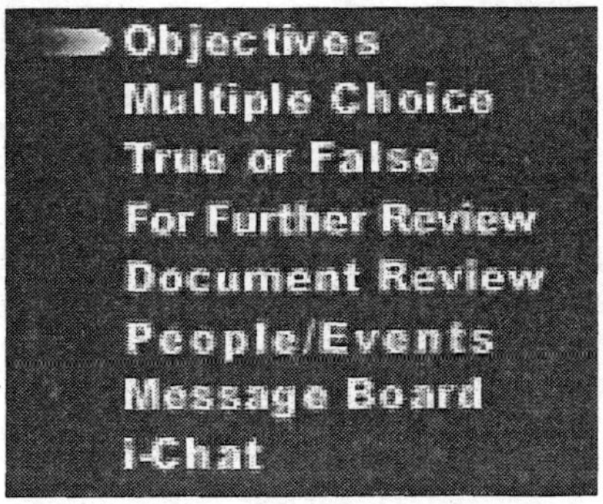

Figure 11. The middle of the navigation bar provides links directly to the quiz, research, and communication modules.

The bottom portion of the navigation bar (Figure 12) contains links to the Help files, User Profile, Feedback, Site Search, and Course Syllabus, if available.

Figure 12. The bottom portion of the navigation bar contains links to the help files, user profile, feedback, site search, and course syllabus.

Section 4
The Modules

Objectives

The opening page of every chapter defines the unit by providing a summary of the topics covered. This summary can be a list of learning goals for the chapter, a brief introduction/overview of the chapter, or a combination of the two formats.

Multiple Choice

As in traditional learning environments, *Multiple Choice* quizzes are one of the most popular methods of online testing. In fact, the majority of Prentice Hall Companion Websites include at least one *Multiple Choice* quiz. Depending on which book you are using, this quiz module may have a name other than "Multiple Choice." Sample names range from "Review I" to "Elements."

1. Which of the following best defines psychology?

○ the science of human and animal behavior
○ the science of mental and emotional disorder
○ the study of actions and reactions
○ the scientific study of behavior and mental processes

Figure 13. This is an example of a *Multiple Choice* question.

Figure 13 is from an actual *Multiple Choice* quiz module. Each question consists of the following elements:

- the question.
- a *Hint* that will open in a new, smaller browser window.
- the possible answers.

In order to select an answer, mark the circle in front of it with your mouse. When you have completed the quiz, click on the *Submit for Grade* button at the bottom of the page to send your answers to the *Results Reporter* (see page 14).

True or False

True or False quizzes are another popular feature of Companion Websites. Depending on the book you are using, this module may have a name other than "True or False."

1. The term "mind" in modern-day psychology refers only to conscious mental states.

o FALSE
o TRUE

Figure 14. This is an example of a True or False question.

Figure 14 is an example from an actual *True or False* quiz module. Each question consists of the following elements:

- the question.
- a *Hint* that will open in a new, smaller browser window.
- the two possible answers.

In order to select an answer, mark the circle in front of it with your mouse. When you have completed the quiz, click on the *Submit for Grade* button at the bottom of the page to send your answers to the *Results Reporter* (see page 14).

Fill in the Blanks

Depending on which book you are using, this quiz module may have a name other than "Fill in the Blanks."

1. When preconceptions influence our observations and our questions about a matter, we are showing a _____.

o deviation
o attribution
o placebo effect
o bias

Figure 15. This is an example of a *Fill in the Blanks* question. Its format is the same as a traditional *Multiple Choice* question.

Figure 15 is from an actual *Fill in the Blanks* quiz module. Each question consists of the following elements:

- the question with a blank line.
- a *Hint* that will open in a new, smaller browser window.
- a list of possible answers that could fill in the blank line.

In order to select an answer, mark the circle in front of it with your mouse. When you have completed the quiz, click on the *Submit for Grade* button at the bottom of the page to send your answers to the *Results Reporter* (see page 14).

Essay

Depending on the book you are using, this quiz module may have a name other than Essay. Some examples include "Historical Content" and "Journal Assignment." *Essay* modules may contain a block of introductory text and/or images before the questions.

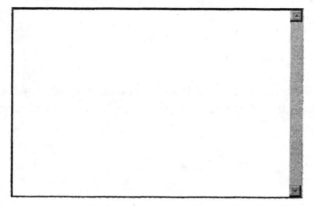

1. Let's do some detective work. Reread the description of Kreskin's transmission of numbers (pg. 2-3). Read it very carefully. How many numbers did Kreskin include among those that he said he would transmit? Write down all the possible numbers that Kreskin could transmit, according to his statement to the audience.

Figure 16. This is an example of an *Essay* question.

Figure 16 is from an actual *Essay* module. Each question consists of the following elements:

- a question.
- an optional *Hint* that will open in a new, smaller browser window.
- a large box, in which you type (or cut-and-paste from another application) your essay.

When you have completed the quiz, click on the *Submit for Grade* button at the bottom of the page to send your answers to the *Results Reporter* (see page 14). Essay questions have to be manually graded by your instructor, but the *Results Reporter* will tell which questions you answered and may give you some general feedback.

Pattern Match

Pattern Match is the newest addition to the Companion Website question library. Although similar in format to traditional *Fill in the Blanks* questions, *Pattern Match* eliminates the list of possible choices, forcing you to generate your own answer. Depending on what book you are using, this quiz module may have a name other than "Pattern Match."

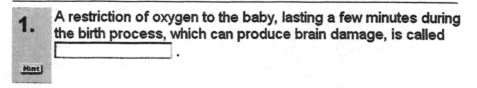

1. A restriction of oxygen to the baby, lasting a few minutes during the birth process, which can produce brain damage, is called _____ .

Figure 17. This is an example of a *Pattern Match* question.

Figure 17 is from a *Pattern Match* quiz module. Each question consists of the following elements:

- the question.
- a *Hint* that will open in a new, smaller browser window.
- a text entry box.

To enter an answer, click your cursor within the box and begin typing. When you have completed the quiz, click on the *Submit for Grade* button at the bottom of the page to send your answers to the *Results Reporter* (see page 14).

Labeling

Labeling exercises consist of images with letters that correspond to specific areas. To identify the areas, you select terms from a list below the image. Depending on which book you are using, this quiz module may have a name other than "Labeling."

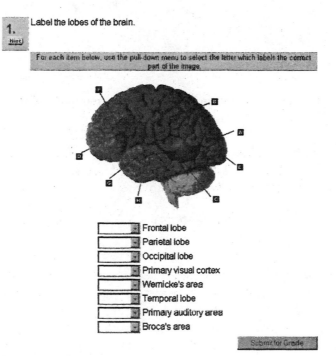

Figure 18. This is an example of a *Labeling* question.

Figure 18 is from a *Labeling* quiz module. To answer the questions:

- Read the introductory text. Click on the *Hint* link if you need some help. *Hints* will open in a new, smaller browser window.
- Examine the image.
- After reading the terms or descriptions, use the pull-down menus to select the letter that corresponds with the text to the right of the menu.

When you have completed the quiz, click on the *Submit for Grade* button at the bottom of the page to send your answers to the *Results Reporter* (see page 14).

Results Reporter

Once you have submitted your work through the *Submit* button, your answers are passed to the automatic grader and your grades are displayed in the *Results Reporter*. This section will explain what each part of the *Results Reporter* displays.

The first part of the *Results Reporter* summarizes how you did, beginning with the percentage of questions you answered correctly (in Figure 19, 70%). You are also shown graphically how many questions you answered correctly and/or incorrectly, as well as the number of questions you didn't answer. Sometimes, the *Results Reporter* will include information about the amount of time you took to complete the quiz. The grading of *Essay* modules cannot be automated so the *Results Reporter* will only display a listing of how many questions you answered.

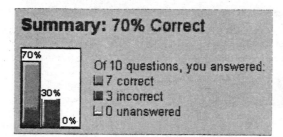

Figure 19. The first part of the *Results Reporter* summarizes how you did, beginning with the percentage of questions you answered correctly. You are also shown graphically how many questions you answered correctly and/or incorrectly, as well as the number of questions you didn't answer.

The bulk of the *Results Reporter* is a question-by-question examination of your responses which looks like this:

1. Incorrect   Marriage forms are similar across social and cultural groups.
                  Your Answer: TRUE
                  The correct answer: FALSE

                  The correct answer is FALSE because marriage forms vary across societal and cultural groups (see p. 2).

The top line shows the question number, whether you got the answer Correct or Incorrect, and the text of the question. Next, the *Results Reporter* lists **Your answer** and **The correct answer**. Finally, depending upon the book you are using, the report may include an explanation of why your answer was correct or incorrect and where to look for additional information in your textbook.

At the bottom of the *Results Reporter* screen you can enter contact information for the people to whom you would like to send your grades (Figure 20). If your recipients prefer to receive your results in the body of an e-mail message, select either "as plain text" or "as HTML" (for Netscape or *Explorer* e-mail). On the other hand, if your recipients prefer to receive your results as an attachment, select either "as text attachment" or "as HTML attachment" (for *Navigator* or *Explorer* e-mail). Please note that you should always e-mail yourself a copy of your results because Prentice Hall will not save a back-up copy.

As discussed earlier, the *Profile* feature lets you standardize the submission of your quiz results. By (carefully) entering your personal information in this screen, you can avoid retyping it every time you need to submit homework. Once saved, the information will appear automatically whenever it's required.

Remember that you MUST click on the *E-mail Results* button at the bottom of the *Results Reporter* each time you want to send results to an instructor.

Routing Information

You may pre-set these fields, and choose other e-mail preferences by clicking the "Your Profile" button at left.

My name is:

[   ]

E-mail my results to:

	E-mail address:	Send as:
Me:	[ ]	[Text ▾]
Instructor:	[ ]	[Text ▾]
TA:	[ ]	[Text ▾]
Other:	[ ]	[Text ▾]

[E-Mail Results]

Figure 20. By filling out this form you not only select the recipients of your quiz results, but you also select the format of your messages.

Destinations

This module contains a list of Internet resources relevant to the work in your course. Depending on which book you are using, this module may have a name other than "Destinations." Common titles include "Web Destinations" and "Online Resources."

Each *Destinations* entry will look like this:

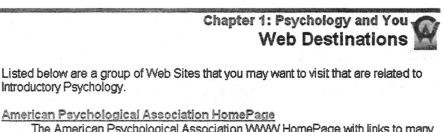

Chapter 1: Psychology and You
Web Destinations

Listed below are a group of Web Sites that you may want to visit that are related to Introductory Psychology.

American Psychological Association HomePage
The American Psychological Association WWW HomePage with links to many other pertinent interests in psychology. Great for new and experienced psychology students alike.

Please note that these resources generally link to sites outside of Prentice Hall. To visit a particular site, click on the underlined word or phrase (the hypertext link). This link will open a new, smaller browser window containing the information you requested. When finished with the link, return to your Companion Website by closing the smaller window.

Net Search

Net Search allows you to search the Internet based on keywords specified in each Companion Website chapter. Depending on the book you are using, this module may have a name other than "Net Search."

Figure 21 is from a *Net Search* module. To use *Net Search*:

- Read the introductory text, which may include specific instructions or other guidance on how to conduct a search for the terms listed.
- Click on one or more keywords from the list of terms. The term or terms will be added to the empty text box. You can also type in terms of your own or add Boolean operators, such as AND, NOT, OR, +, etc.
- Select a search engine from the pull-down menu.
- Click on the *Search* button to execute your search.

If your search doesn't yield the results you desire, select another one of the search engines from the pull-down menu and try again.

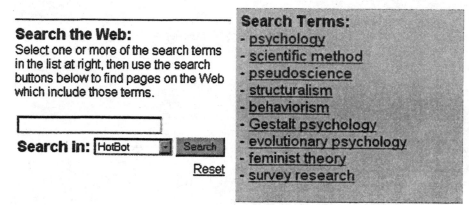

Figure 21. *Net Search* allows you to search the Internet based on keywords specified in each Companion Website chapter.

Message Board
Prentice Hall Message Boards use browser technology to provide students and instructors with a national forum to discuss topics related to their studies.

Configuring Your Browser for Prentice Hall Message Boards
If your system is configured correctly, when you access a Prentice Hall Message Board through a Companion Website, you will already be viewing the virtual bulletin board in your browser. If this is not the case, you are probably configured incorrectly. See the *Online Help* files for instructions on configuring your software.

Reading Messages
Upon entering the message board (Figure 22), you will see a list of messages in the lower portion of the screen. If there are replies to a message, they will be presented in a hierarchy that displays the reply structure. To see this hierarchy, click on the plus side on the *All* button or on the small green arrows next to the subject titles. Groups of related messages are commonly called *threads* of conversation.

Subject ▼	Sender ▼	Date ▼
No Subject	Doe, Anonymous	12/18/98 01:28 PM
▷2301-090 with prof crane	Doe, Anonymous	01/12/99 06:40 PM
pysc 2301-90 prof crane	kingsbury, lisa	01/22/99 12:15 PM
quiz	Doe, Anonymous	02/07/99 10:58 PM
Class Project	Doe, Anonymous	02/13/99 10:11 PM
No Subject	Doe, Anonymous	02/22/99 01:02 PM
▷Psyc6170-01	Guimaraes, Debora	03/01/99 02:06 PM
▷Downloads	Becker, Catherine	03/02/99 12:02 PM
▷6170	Sexton, Ginna	03/05/99 10:45 AM
6170-01	Baptista, Niosoty	03/09/99 06:27 PM

Figure 22. Upon entering the message board, you will see a list of messages in the lower portion of the screen.

Click on a subject title, and the message will appear in the lower window of the browser above a navigation bar (Figure 23). Use the buttons to read through the messages in a conversation, move to another thread, or return to the main list of postings.

From: Jacob Schwartz

Date: 04/13/99 03:15 PM

Subject: Ch. 6: memory

Message: Does anyone know the difference between Episodal Memory and Auto-Biographical memory? They sound like the same thing. Thanx. Jacob Schwartz jwschwartz@juno.com

◀◀	◀	▲	▶	▶▶
previous thread	previous message	back to threaded list	next message	next thread

Figure 23. Messages appear in the lower window above a navigation bar.

To post a message, select the *Post New Message* button above the main index of messages (Figure 23). When the form opens in the lower frame (Figure 24), enter your name, subject title, and message in the appropriate fields. When you are finished, click on the *Done – Post Message* button to post your comments to the message board. You can leave this screen at any time by clicking the *Cancel* button.

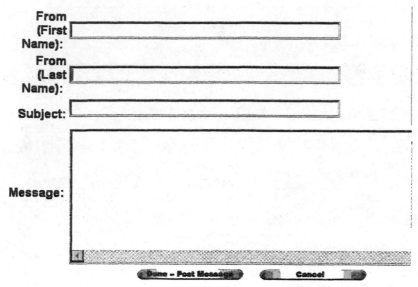

Figure 24. To post a message to a message board, click on the *Post New Message* button.

To encourage discussion and debate, your reply to an existing message can be associated with an original posting. In order to do this, view the message to which you would like to respond and click on the *Reply to Message* button in the upper left-hand corner of the window (Figure 23). You will be presented with a window similar to the form for creating new messages, but the *Subject* field will be automatically generated (Figure 25). Enter your name and message in the appropriate fields. When you are finished, click on the *Done – Post Message* button to post your comments to the message board. You can leave this screen at any time by clicking the *Cancel* button.

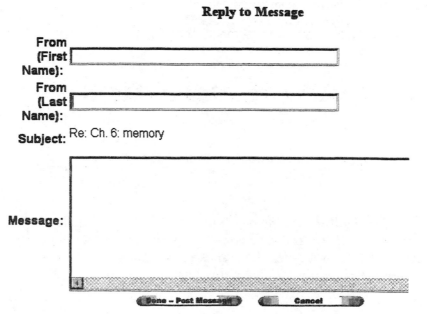

Figure 25. When replying to a message, the Subject field will be automatically generated.

i-Chat

I-Chat not only allows instructors to host private class discussions, invite guest speakers to class, and reach students easily, but it also gives you the opportunity to meet students from around the world. In order to gain full functionality of Prentice Hall chat rooms, we recommend that you use the *i-Chat* plug-in. If you choose not to do so, *i-Chat* is also accessible using Java or HTML clients (your browser will automatically select the client that provides the most features).

To enter *i-Chat*:

- Download the *i-Chat* plug-in (accessible from our tune-up page).
- Click on the *i-Chat* button on your Companion Website navigation bar.
- Enter a nickname for yourself.
- Select your chat type. We recommend the default setting.
- Click on the *Enter Chat Area* button.

Although the top region may contain some introductory text or instructions, the bottom region is the actual *i-Chat* client area (Figure 26). Your name and the name of the other users will appear in this area as will the text of the chat. At the bottom of the chat client area, you will find the text entry area. You can begin to participate by simply typing a message into this region and pressing *Enter*.

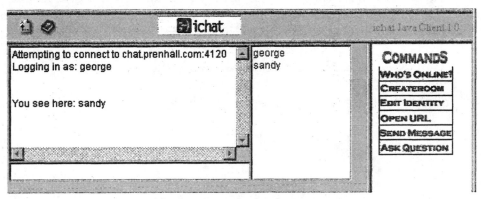

Figure 26. At the bottom of the chat client area, you will find the text entry area. You can begin to participate by simply typing a message into this region and pressing *Enter*.

Once you've mastered the basics of chatting, you may want to experiment with the additional menu choices available. For help when you are in *i-chat*, use the help icon that resembles a book with a question mark.

Advanced i-Chat Features

Sending Private Messages.   Private messages can be sent to individual users through the client menu bar. Click on the icon of the person in silhouette. A new window asking for the recipient and the private message will be generated.

Creating a Private Room for Your Online Study Group.   Private rooms can also be set up for discussions limited to only a few people. One member of the group should create the room using the *Create Private Room* option under the *Commands* sub-menu of the chat menu. Fill out the form requesting a private room. If you have a URL you would like to display in the banner, type it in the URL field; otherwise you can use a default URL such as **http://www.prenhall.com**. In order for others to join you in the room, you have to invite them by using the */invite {username}* command.

The room will be removed when all participants have left. Private rooms can be exited by using the Navigation sub-menu of the chat menu, or by using the */go {exitname}* command.

Groups

Groups can have many names, but their basic premise is to gather several quiz, research, or communication modules into one area, thereby reducing clutter on the navigation bar. Figure 27 is an example of a group that contains several quizzes. Typical groups contain navigation icons and some instructions.

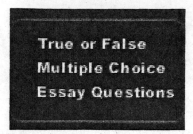

Figure 27. This is an example of a group of modules. Note that the icons work just like the ones in the main navigation bar.

Other Modules

Because technology changes rapidly, you may encounter modules in a Companion Website that are not covered in this book. Most often the URLs for such modules will contain the words "custom.html." As Prentice Hall introduces new technologies to Companion Websites, helpful instructions will be incorporated within the modules as well as within the online *Help* pages. If you can't find an answer to your problems within these pages, please contact Prentice Hall's help support staff via e-mail:

web_tech_support@prenhall.com

To help in answering your questions quickly, please carefully describe your problem(s) and the browser you are using.

Guide to The Psychology Place™

A wealth of content is available to you in *The Psychology Place*. To make it easy for you to see what we have, we've provided a Quick Reference section that gives you a bird's-eye view of the categories and articles available for each chapter. This is followed by a lengthier set of annotations so you can see what each article covers.

Learning Activities

The faculty and publisher of *The Psychology Place* are committed to providing rich and varied learning activities that promote inquiry-based learning on the Web. You will find investigative activities that explore core concepts, research, and current topics related to your introductory psychology course. Online labs and experiments allow you to collect and compare data with other students. You will participate in interactive tutorials and exercises that challenge your critical thinking skills in important, everyday decisions.

Research News

These articles provide psychology's perspective on real-life events and keep you up-to-date on interesting research that is being done all over the world. Explore information related to your course or find materials for research projects. Each Research News article includes print and Web references that can be used for further research.

Op Ed Essays

The Op Ed Essays are written by guest contributors and challenge us with important new information, ideas, or strategies pertinent to introductory psychology. They are interactive as well, and you are invited to join a collegial dialogue about the issues raised by the contributors.

Scientific American Connection

The Scientific American Connection provides a collection of articles from *Scientific American* magazine selected based on their relevance to introductory psychology. These articles are specially reformatted for the Web and include links to our glossary and to additional Web resources.

Ask Dr. Mike

Got a question about psychology? Well, you've come to the right place! After 15 years of teaching introductory psychology, Dr. Mike Atkinson has heard them all and in this space has provided answers to the most frequently-asked questions.

The Psychology Place
Quick Reference Guide

	Learning Activities	Research News	Op Ed Essays	Ask Dr. Mike
Chapter One **Psychology, Research, and You**	Exploring Arguments: Deciding What to Believe Critical Thinking: I Know It's a Good Thing, but What Is It? Product Claims: Too Good to be True? Caveat Emptor: Evaluating Knowledge Claims Searching the Web: Investigating Alzheimer's Disease	Animal Rights Activists: Changing Views on Animal Research Drawing Conclusions: The Child Sexual Abuse Controversy Is Embarrassment a Distinct Emotion?	What Questions are on Psychologists' Minds Today? How Did Leading Psychologists Find Psychology? Building a Prototype of Master Teaching: Finding Common Ground Building Partnerships in Psychology to Enhance Teaching and Learning What are the Implications of National Standards for Teaching Psychology?	What's the difference between a psychologist and a psychiatrist? What are psychologists most interested in regarding behavior? Do I need to go to medical school for a career in research psychology? I'm confused about independent and dependent variables. Can you help? In order to go to graduate school in psychology, do I need to get a B.A. or a B.S.? In the Milgram experiment, why didn't the participants just leave? Aren't you free to leave a study at any time? Is it true that Freud was addicted to cocaine? My textbook seems to have a LOT of information. How do I know what's important? What does p <.05 mean? Please help! What is a "placebo"? What is APA style? Can you give some examples? What is factor analysis? I'm lost! What kind of grades do you need in high school to be a psychologist, and what classes should you take? What's the difference between a random sample and random assignment?

	Learning Activities	Research News	Op Ed Essays	Ask Dr. Mike
				When writing in APA style, is it okay to put a running head in question form?
				Who is the most "famous" psychologist?
Chapter Two **Biological Foundations of Psychology** **Scientific American Connection**	Action at the Synapse Investigating the Evolutionary Perspective: 3 Dads and a Baby	Second Languages and the Brain: New Organization for Later Learners Cockroach Pheromones Can Cause Social Dominance Sex Alters the Brain Prenatal Experience: More is Not Better Evolutionary Change Before Your Eyes Planum Temporale: Brain Structure Behind Language Evolution? Brain Area Represents Local Visual Environments How the Brain "Hears" Sign Language Adult Brains Can Generate New Neurons Early Pain Influences the Development of the Nervous System Glia: The Forgotten Majority Leptin: Weight Loss Panacea or Pipe Dream? Pavlonian Conditioning and Meals Seeing with Your Auditory Cortex Steroids Elicit Manic Symptoms Superman, Spinal Damage, and Stem Cell The Shape of Beauty: In the Eye of the Beholder?	The Mathematics of Beauty	Does the research on "split-brain" patients suggest a basis for the unconscious? Is the left hemisphere conscious, while the right is unconscious? What is the cause of ambidexterity? What is an antihistamine and how does it work? What if a neuron doesn't have enough "firing power?" What does all of this physiological stuff have to do with psychology? Brain tumor? What are some of the side effects? And if you have surgery, what are the chances of not having anything wrong with that person? What's the difference between an action potential and a graded potential? What is actually measured when someone measures your "arousal level?" Are couples who have twins more likely to have twins again? Are there any differences between the male and female brain? Can the smaller Y chromosome be considered genetically "inferior" to the larger X chromosome? I've heard people use the term "crackpot" for someone who was crazy. Where does this term come from? I've heard that Prozac has few, if any, side effects. Is this true?

	Learning Activities	Research News	Op Ed Essays	Ask Dr. Mike
				If eye color is the result of a dominant (brown) allele and a recessive (blue) allele, how can you have green eyes? Using a Mendel table, the color should be either brown or blue, shouldn't it?
				If the neurotransmitter serotonin enhances mood, how is it related to depression?
				Is alcoholism genetic?
				Is it true that people with PKU can't drink milk?
				Is lithium the only drug treatment for bipolar disorder?
				Is there a chemical in turkey that makes you sleepy?
				Is there a greater tendency for homosexuals to be left-handed?
				What are the effects of PCP on the brain?
				What are the major neurotransmitters and their functions?
				What do you think may be the next most important discovery about the brain?
				What does the spleen do?
				What is a "split-brain" procedure?
				What is a migraine headache?
				What is dysgraphia?
				What is serotonin?
				What is THC and how does it work?
				Why does psychology favor Darwin's theory of evolution over creationism?

	Learning Activities	Research News	Op Ed Essays	Ask Dr. Mike
Chapter Three **Sensation and Perception**	Investigating Depth Perception Investigating Olfaction: The Nose Knows	Seeing with Your Auditory Cortex Brain Area Represents Local Visual Environments Auditory Perceptual Deficits in Language-Impaired Children		How do you explain those "magic eye" 3D pictures? What happens when your eye becomes "bloodshot?" Are carrots good for your eyesight? Do cartoons appear to move through the autokinetic effect? Young infants seem to show a preference for looking at faces. Could this be due to the fact that faces are the only things they've seen in the delivery room? When older people begin to have problems with their vision, does this have anything to do with damage to the visual cortex? Can you explain Fechner's Law? Does time really go faster as you get older? How can we perceive dreams as visual images since we sleep with eyes closed and the receptors are not firing? How does acupuncture work? How would a behaviorist explain the operation of an aphrodisiac? I know that the moon can't really be bigger when it's just rising, but it looks that way. Why? I'm always confused by the terms "nearsighted" and "farsighted." In which is your vision good for close objects? Is sense of smell different in females and males? What actually happens during laser eye surgery? What causes dyslexia? What is synesthesia?

	Learning Activities	Research News	Op Ed Essays	Ask Dr. Mike
				What is THC and how does it work?
				What is the visual system, what is color vision, and what are the differences in color vision among different species? And what does any of this have to do with psychology?
				Why can you sometimes still see flashing lights or "spots" after you shut your eyes?
				Why do we see impossible images?
				Why do you sometimes feel that the eyes of a person in a painting are "following" you?
				Why do your ears get "blocked" and "pop" when landing in an airplane?
Chapter Four **Motivation and Emotion** **Scientific American Connection**	Exploring Academic Dishonesty Emotion, Memory and the Brain	Is Embarrassment a Distinct Emotion? Should Creativity Be Rewarded? Giving Children Rewards: A Right Way and a Wrong Way		When I get angry, why does my chest start to hurt? What is a "lie detector?" Do animals imitate? If so, what does this mean? Can a polygraph really determine whether or not you're lying? How could I do a demonstration on lying in the classroom? Does alcohol really kill brain cells? How would a behaviorist explain the operation of an aphrodisiac? I have been on Prozac for about 6 to 8 months now, and I have been having very violent and disturbing dreams. Could this be a side effect of the Prozac? Is catharsis a good thing or a bad thing? I've heard both. Is there any evidence to suggest that homosexuality is due to "nature" rather than "nurture"? My friend and I have bet and hope you can settle it for us. Who is better at lying, men or women?

	Learning Activities	Research News	Op Ed Essays	Ask Dr. Mike
				What can you tell me about Rohypnol?
				What is actually measured when someone measures your "arousal level"?
				What is emotional intelligence? Is it the same thing as IQ?
				What is narcolepsy? And can narcolepsy affect your sex life?
				Why do people yawn?
				Why does a moth fly toward a light?
				Why is it that sometimes people think you're lying when you're not lying at all?
Chapter Five **States of Consciousness** **Scientific American Connection**	Drug Use, Abuse, and Addictions: Focus on Alcohol Investigating Dreams	Cigarette Smoking and Genetics: A Not So Unlikely Combination One Eye Open: How Sleeping Ducks Avoid Becoming "Sitting Ducks" Psychoactive Drugs for Children: Panacea or Peril? Scientists Battle Nicotine The Secret to Better Grades Might Be More Sleep	Are We Chronically Sleep-Deprived? A Harmful Psychoactive Drug for Children	What is THC and how does it work? Is it possible to walk or act out behavior while dreaming? If you dream that you are falling and if you hit the ground, will you die? Can dreams predict the future? How do you explain the fact that sometimes you dream about something and then it happens? How do you figure out that a particular symbol stands for something else in a dream? We have been talking a lot in class about ESP. What is your opinion on this subject? Are dreams and visions something to worry about? Do they affect our lives in any way? Can learning occur "unconsciously" as suggested in "learn while you sleep" tapes? Can reinforcement be presented "subconsciously"? Can we learn without being aware? Can we control our dreams?

	Learning Activities	Research News	Op Ed Essays	Ask Dr. Mike
				Can you become addicted to the Internet?
				Can you practice to have a lucid dream? How?
				Do people in comas dream?
				Does everyone dream? If not, why?
				If a person snores, does this mean that they have a mild case of sleep apnea?
				Is alcoholism genetic?
				Is there a chemical in turkey that makes you sleepy?
				I've heard that Seasonal Affective Disorder (SAD) is caused by a lack of sunlight, but is it also related to temperature?
				My textbook says that serotonin is an inhibitory neurotransmitter. It also says that LSD blocks serotonin receptor sites, implying that LSD is an antagonist (as the inhibitory effects of serotonin are blocked). Yet in the Psychology Place, Kolb and Wishaw (1996) are cited as describing LSD as an agonist. What is LSD, agonist or antagonist, and why?
				We have been talking a lot in class about ESP. What is your opinion on this subject?
				What are the effects of PCP on the brain?
				What are the long-term risks of taking the drug Adderall?
				What can you tell me about Rohypnol?
				What can you tell me about the drug, "ecstasy"?
				What is narcolepsy? And can narcolepsy affect your sex life?
				Why do people yawn?

	Learning Activities	Research News	Op Ed Essays	Ask Dr. Mike
Chapter Six **Basic Principles of Learning**	Principles of Learning in the Real World	Songbird Brain Cell Count Predicts Learning Giving Children Rewards: A Right Way and a Wrong Way Beyond Pavlov's Dogs Should Creativity Be Rewarded? Numerical Ability in Chimpanzees Pavlovian Conditioning and Meals		If you punish a response (e.g., bar pressing), what happens when you no longer deliver the punishment? In a counterconditioning procedure, can you get a transfer of fear to the positive stimulus rather than the other way around? Can reinforcement be presented "unconsciously?" Can we learn without being aware? My students have a tough time in distinguishing between negative reinforcement and punishment. What are some good examples of each? In Pavlov's studies, wouldn't he have trouble controlling the dogs as soon as they entered the experimental room? Wouldn't they learn to salivate at the sight and sound of the door? How would a behaviorist explain the operation of an aphrodisiac? I've heard that aluminum may cause Alzheimer's Disease. Should I worry about drinking from aluminum cans? My dog has severe reactions to thunderstorms. He shakes, pants, and appears to be in a state of panic. Lately he reacts the same way to cars, trucks, and even rain on the roof. The vet prescribed an antianxiety medicine, but is there a nonmedical way to treat my dog? What's the difference between desensitization, counterconditioning, and aversive conditioning? When a person develops a taste aversion but doesn't remember the incident surrounding the aversion, how is this explained in terms of classical conditioning?

	Learning Activities	Research News	Op Ed Essays	Ask Dr. Mike
Chapter Seven **Memory** **Scientific American Connection**	Product Claims: Too Good to be True? Test Your Memory	The Repressed Memory Debate Another Measure of Intelligence: Working Memory The Secret to Better Grades Might Be More Sleep	Recovered-memory Experiences: Explaining True and False Delayed Memories of Childhood Sexual Abuse	If the proper cue could be found, would it be possible to retrieve any memory? Is any particular type of music related to memory recall in positive or negative ways? How and why? Can the environmental context influence memory? Does dementia lead to Alzheimer's disease or is it a separate disorder? Is there a way to measure a person's memory span? Since we can get primacy and recency effects for memory, does this mean that it is better to study in smaller chunks, taking breaks? What is Ginkgo? Does it improve memory? What is synesthesia?
Chapter Eight **Thinking and Intelligence**	Understanding Mental Models Critical Thinking: I Know It's a Good Thing, but What Is It? Making Sound Decisions: The Worksheet Method Product Claims: Too Good to be True?	The Growing Popularity of "Emotional Intelligence" Auditory Perceptual Deficits in Language-Impaired Children Planum Temporale: Brain Structure Behind Language Evolution? Another Explanation for Differences in Intellectual Performance: Stereotype Threat How the Brain "Hears" Sign Language Babies, Phonetics, and Mastering Language Second Languages and the Brain: New Organization for Later Learners Another Measure of Intelligence: Working Memory How Stereotypes Affect Test Performance		What is the "Chitterling Test?" What causes dyslexia? What is Savant Syndrome and what causes it? If savants are so good at counting, why can't they make change for $1.00? Can your IQ level change over time? Is the term "mentally retarded" still acceptable? Are there really racial differences in intelligence? Can you explain cognition in a manner that a child would understand? Does group size affect the quality of decision making? If smaller groups make better decisions, why do we have juries composed of 12 people? How can I tell how many morphemes there are in a word?

	Learning Activities	Research News	Op Ed Essays	Ask Dr. Mike
				If you administered both the Stanford-Binet test and the WISC test to the same person, would you derive the same IQ score?
				Is it true that playing music to a baby while it is still in the womb can increase the child's intelligence?
				Should the Stanford-Binet scale be changed over time since children's abilities are probably changing?
				What does a score of 90 on an IQ test mean?
				What is dysgraphia?
				What is the distinction between Thurstone's theory of intelligence and that offered by Sternberg?
				Why do child prodigies, or highly gifted children, burn out so quickly or never really make it in the real world?
Chapter Nine **Developmental Psychology I: Conception Through Childhood**	Tick Tock Goes the Social and Biological Clock Investigating the Evolutionary Perspective: 3 Dads and a Baby	Daycare: What's a Parent to Do? Birth Month Predicts Height? Babies, Phonetics, and Mastering Language Infant Attachment, Adult Curiosity, and Cognitive Closure Childhood Attachment Style: How Stable Over the Life Span? Should Parents Intervene in Children's Fights? Even Light Maternal Drinking Affects the Unborn Child Attention Deficit Disorder— A Potential Advantage Child Development: The Neighborhood Effect Drawing Conclusions: The Child Sexual Abuse Controversy Is a Male Role Model Essential to Positive Child Development? Nature vs. Nurture: Genes Win Again!	Challenging the Nurture Assumption The Power of Parents Children's Private Speech: Meaningless Chatter or Essential Tool?	What is a "critical period?" If a mother smokes during pregnancy, are there any effects on the fetus? Is "Motherese" universal— does this appear in all cultures? Do young children have a conscience? What are the causes of various attachment styles? Is it the parent's behavior or the child's? If eye color is the result of a dominant (brown) allele and a recessive (blue) allele, how can you have green eyes? Using a Mendel table, the color should be either brown or blue, shouldn't it? To what extent does the lack of infant attachment adversely influence adult behavior?

	Learning Activities	Research News	Op Ed Essays	Ask Dr. Mike
				If attachment is strong and secure at an early age, what happens when you move out on your own? Do you have to replace this secure attachment?
				We recently saw the videotape entitled "Secret of the Wild Child." This was a NOVA special featuring the unique story of the young girl who was found in California in the early 1970s after having endured almost total social isolation. My students and I were curious to know where and how Genie is today. Could you tell us what became of her?
				Are couples who have twins more likely to have twins again?
				Can the smaller Y chromosome be considered genetically "inferior" to the larger X chromosome?
				Does violence on TV make children do violent things? Do children get ideas from TV or do they think what they see on TV is real?
				Is TV violence getting worse?
				Is walking at an early age a sign of future athletic ability?
				I've heard that in the first moments of life a baby should be held by its mother in order for bonding to occur. Is this true?
				What's the first word that an infant learns?
				Whom do babies resemble more, their mothers or their fathers? My sister just had a baby boy and he looks exactly like she did in her baby pictures.

	Learning Activities	Research News	Op Ed Essays	Ask Dr. Mike
Chapter Ten **Developmental Psychology II: Adolescence Through Old Age** **Scientific American Connection**	Tick Tock Goes the Social and Biological Clock Searching the Web: Investigating Alzheimer's Disease	Teen Suicide—Symptom of a Changing World or Exaggerated Suggestibility in Adolescence? Fear of Death: Our Final Developmental Crisis Primate Caretakers Live Longer Regrets? . . . I've Had a Few: Women's Midlife Review and Well-Being Sharing Secrets: Siblings and Self-Disclosure Successful Aging: A Matter of Control?	Who or What is to Blame for the Littleton Massacre? Challenging the Nurture Assumption The Power of Parents The Tragedy of Adolescent Suicide—Finding Options for Prevention	Did TV violence cause the Littleton situation? Does dementia lead to Alzheimer's disease or is it a separate disorder? I read an article recently where they said that having a "wet dream" was a normal experience and did not reflect a psychological disorder. Is this true or does it really reflect a disorder? Recently, I shared with my AP Psychology class a videotape entitled "Secret of the Wild Child." This was a NOVA special featuring the unique story of the young girl who was found in California in the early 1970s after having endured almost total social isolation. My students and I were curious to know where and how Genie is today. Could you tell us what became of her?
Chapter Eleven **Sex and Gender** **Scientific American Connection**	Investigating Sex Differences in Depression	Eating Disorders and Sudden Death Scent of a Woman: The Scientific Sequel Does Being Female Increase Depression Risks for Females? The Shape of Beauty: In the Eye of the Beholder?		What does Freud have to say about the development of homosexuality in men? Are there any differences between the male and female brain? I read an article recently where they said that having a "wet dream" was a normal experience and did not reflect a psychological disorder. Is this true or does it really reflect a disorder? Is there any evidence to suggest that homosexuality is due to "nature" rather than "nurture"? My friend and I have a bet and hope you can settle it for us. Who is better at lying, men or women?

	Learning Activities	Research News	Op Ed Essays	Ask Dr. Mike
Chapter Twelve **Personality**	Investigating Graphology: Is the Writing on the Wall? Investigating Dreams		Who or What is to Blame for the Littleton Massacre? The Social Usefulness of Self-Esteem: A Skeptical View	What are ink blots made out of and how are they made? In the Freudian structure of the mind, is it fair to say that the Id is "selfish," and that the Superego is "good?" Can a personality test ever be "wrong"? I've heard that aluminum may cause Alzheimer's Disease. Should I worry about drinking from aluminum cans? What's a "Freudian slip"? Where can I find various personality inventories on the Web?
Chapter Thirteen **Psychological Disorders** **Scientific American Connection**	Investigating Sex Differences in Depression Recognizing Mood Disorders Drug Use, Abuse, and Addictions: Focus on Alcohol	Editor's Note: Unabomber Update Schizophrenic Disorder: When People Hear Voices, Who's Talking? Eating Disorders and Sudden Death Mental Illness: Dangers, Treatment, and Civil Liberties The Manic-Depressive Brain DSM-IV: How Many Entries for The Book of Names? Teen Suicide—Symptom of a Changing World or Exaggerated Suggestibility in Adolescence? The Insanity Defense and the Unabomber Trial Beyond Shyness: Diagnosing and Treating Social Phobia Does Being Female Increase Depression Risks for Females? Gambling as an Addictive Disorder Prescription for Depression and PMS: Sleep Deprivation? Understanding Schizophrenia: Where and When You Were Born Makes a Difference	The Tragedy of Adolescent Suicide—Finding Options for Prevention	What is antisocial personality disorder? Can this explain the Littleton shootings? What is an "anxiety attack?" What is bipolar disease, and how do you get it? What are some symptoms, and is there a cure? Can psychological blindness correct itself? What is Tourette's Syndrome? What is "normal," anyway? If reality is based on perception, how can we label a schizophrenic as "abnormal?" Is it typical to feel "down" after reading or talking about depression? What is the likelihood that the genes for a mental disorder can be passed down from your parents? Would the home environment have any effect? With multiple personality disorder, can one of the personalities be ill while the other is healthy?

	Learning Activities	Research News	Op Ed Essays	Ask Dr. Mike
				Concerning Tourette's Syndrome, does a person have inappropriate behaviors other than swearing, such as inappropriate sexual behavior in public?
				Is Anorexia Nervosa really a form of Anxiety Disorder?
				What is Luvox?
				Are there any patterns, symptoms, or characteristics of children and wives who are abused?
				Can children develop schizophrenia?
				Can you become addicted to the Internet?
				I have a history of bipolar disorder in my family. How can I tell the difference between everyday mood swings and real disorder?
				I've heard that depression is not a thought disorder. However, if a depressed person considers suicide, isn't that an example of a thought disorder?
				I've heard that Prozac has few, if any, side effects. Is this true?
				If a child is born with a mental disorder, are there fewer folds in the child's brain?
				In dissociative identity disorder, can one personality be "blind" while the others have normal vision?
				Is alcoholism genetic?
				Is it common for autistic children to have one "outstanding" ability?
				Is it considered abnormal to sometimes have feelings of depression and consider suicide?
				Is lithium the only drug treatment for bipolar disorder?
				Is there a relationship between a full moon and mental disorders?

	Learning Activities	Research News	Op Ed Essays	Ask Dr. Mike
				Is there such a thing as borderline personality disorder?
				My boyfriend has schizotypal personality disorder. He is seeing a psychiatrist and is taking an antipsychotic. Do you know of any available treatments other than medication?
				What are conversion disorders? What causes them and how do you treat them?
				What are some of the causes of depression? How can you climb out of depression?
				What causes dyslexia?
				What is dysgraphia?
				What is it called if you are afraid of sex?
				What is narcolepsy? And can narcolepsy affect your sex life?
				What is serotonin?
				What is the difference between psychosis and neurosis?
				What was wrong with Jack Nicholson in the movie, "As Good as It Gets"?
				What's the difference between a neurosis and a psychosis?
Chapter Fourteen **Therapy** **Scientific American Connection**		Feeling Low This Winter? "A Sunny Disposition" May Help Childhood and Adolescent Depression—To Medicate or Not? Beyond Shyness: Diagnosing and Treating Social Phobia Prescription for Depression and PMS: Sleep Deprivation? Psychoactive Drugs for Children: Panacea or Peril?		In a counterconditioning procedure, can you get a transfer of fear to the positive stimulus rather than the other way around? What is Luvox? Is electroconvulsive therapy (ECT) always beneficial? I've heard that Prozac has few, if any, side effects. Is this true? Is it common to mix treatments for various disorders, for example, electroconvulsive therapy (ECT) and lithium?

	Learning Activities	Research News	Op Ed Essays	Ask Dr. Mike
				Can biofeedback help combat depression?
				Can psychological blindness correct itself?
				Does serotonin have an effect on depression? Can it induce self-harm?
				I have been on Prozac for about 6 to 8 months now, and I have been having very violent and disturbing dreams. Could this be a side effect of the Prozac?
				If the neurotransmitter serotonin enhances mood, how is it related to depression?
				Is it true that the person who "invented" the lobotomy was killed by one of his patients?
				Is lithium the only drug treatment for bipolar disorder?
				My boyfriend has schizotypal personality disorder. He is seeing a psychiatrist and is taking an antipsychotic. Do you know of any available treatments other than medication?
				What benefit has amantadine shown in people post TBI?
				What can you tell me about Ritalin?
				What is Gestalt Therapy?
Chapter Fifteen **Health Psychology** **Scientific American Connection**		Classes, Computers, Exams . . . and Beer: College Drinking Coping After Abortion Procrastination May Be Dangerous to Your Health and Performance Getting Old: Better Than You Expect Maternal Grooming: A Lifelong Aid to Stress Reduction? Rethinking the Power of Positive Thinking		Does stress help us to remember information (like phone numbers) or does it make us forget? Can meditation heal? Are cigarette smokers physically and psychologically addicted to smoking? How are they physically addicted? How are they psychologically addicted? Can mental attitude influence a biological disease? Can repeated exposure to stress result in an autoimmune disease?

	Learning Activities	Research News	Op Ed Essays	Ask Dr. Mike
		Cigarette Smoking and Genetics: A Not So Unlikely Combination Does Cigarette Smoking Increase Stress Rather Than Reduce It? Is NYC Dangerous to Your Health? Leptin: Weight Loss Panacea or Pipe Dream? Perils of Hostile Feelings: Heart Disease and an Expanding Waistline Regrets? . . . I've Had a Few: Women's Midlife Review and Well-Being Sharing Secrets: Siblings and Self-Disclosure Social Control: Good and Bad for Your Health Teens at Risk Across Cultures: Sex, Drugs, and AIDS The Shape of Beauty: In the Eye of the Beholder? Why Dieters Fail—They Don't Mind Eating When Their Minds Are Elsewhere Women with Cancer: When the Caregiver Requires Care		I've heard stories that a sexually transmitted disease such as syphilis can make you crazy. Is this true? If so, how does it happen? Is it possible to switch between being a Type A and a Type B personality? It seems to me that people spend a long time looking up at the floor indicators in an elevator. What's going on? What is a migraine headache?
Chapter Sixteen **Social Psychology: The Individual in Society**	Investigating Social Judgments: Expectations, Stereotypes, and the Impressions We're Left With Investigating Gangs and Behavior Exploring Academic Dishonesty	Predicting Our Own Social Behavior Another Explanation for Differences in Intellectual Performance: Stereotype Threat Racism Requires Racial Categorization Juvenile Violence: Why the Mass Murder at Jonesboro, Arkansas? When "Harmless" Flirtation Hurts The Social Consequences of Affirmative Action Can Subliminal Messages Manipulate the Subconscious and Behavior? Even Good People Can Be Moral Hypocrites	A Psychologist Looks at the Death Penalty Are We Sugarcoating Culture? Thinking Critically About the Study of Diversity Organized Religion as a Human Universal The Mathematics of Beauty What Makes a Good Leader?	Did TV violence cause the Littleton situation? Is the unresponsive bystander effect only found in North America? What do people usually say when they are asked why they failed to help at an emergency situation? Is Frosh Week based at least partly on deindividuation? Does conformity play any role in jury decision? Why is timing of the requests so important when using the door-in-the-face technique? During times of international conflict, does prejudice within a single country decrease?

	Learning Activities	Research News	Op Ed Essays	Ask Dr. Mike
		How Stereotypes Affect Test Performance

Random Acts of Hate: Mental Disorder, Economic Conditions, or Organizational Membership?

Social Control: Good and Bad for Your Health

Violent Video Game Play Increases Aggression

We Are All Better Than Average | | Were people obedient in the Milgram study because they somehow believed that the experimenter was "good," and would not let them do something harmful?

What about the effects of watching real violence on TV, for example, on the evening news? Are the results the same as with fictional acts of aggression?

Is altruism related to religion, e.g., would a more religious person be less susceptible to bystander effects?

I've often heard that "opposites attract." Is this true? Are people who are opposite in physical attractiveness likely to get along?

It seems likely that media violence can influence aggression, but why are people "drawn" to media violence? Is this some kind of natural drive?

Are there any differences between individual and group decision making?

Attractiveness is an important factor in changing attitudes. So how do you explain "social marketing"—ads that try to get you to contribute to various causes? The people in these ads are not necessarily attractive.

Do we find a potential mate attractive because we are thinking (unconsciously) about how attractive our children might be?

Does the way a teacher dresses have any effect on how much you respect them?

Does violence on TV make children do violent things? Do children get ideas from TV or do they think what they see on TV is real?

I don't understand Cognitive Dissonance Theory. Can you help? |

	Learning Activities	Research News	Op Ed Essays	Ask Dr. Mike
				If you change an attitude, how long will the change last?
				In the Milgram experiment, why didn't the participants just leave? Aren't you free to leave a study at any time?
				The success of "reality TV" suggests that we enjoy watching real people in extraordinary situations. Why then do we still prefer beautiful people in advertising?
				What is the "small world" effect?
				What is the significance of eye contact in human interaction?
				When considering the effects of watching violence in the media, does the type of violence you watch matter? For example, I was depressed after watching "Saving Private Ryan," but relatively excited after watching "The Matrix."
				Who was Stanley Milgram?
				Why do you sometimes feel that the eyes of a person in a painting are "following" you?
				Would a person, opposed to gambling because of his religion, feel a lot of dissonance if he gambles anyway and loses a lot of money?
Chapter Seventeen **Industrial and Organizational Psychology**		Ingratiation May Be Considered Slimy But It May Have Its Rewards The Social Consequences of Affirmative Action Mentoring in the Workplace: Is It Worth the Effort?	What Makes a Good Leader?	Does conformity play any role in jury decisions?

Chapter One
Psychology, Research, and You

Learning Activities

Exploring Arguments: Deciding What to Believe
Test your critical thinking skills in this activity by Diane Halpern. Analyze persuasive appeals, learn how to identify good reasons and conclusions, and practice the art of analyzing arguments.

Critical Thinking: I Know It's a Good Thing, but What Is It?
This tutorial will help you to review the processes of critical thinking. Examine a few scenarios and test your ability to recognize critical thinking in action.

Product Claims: Too Good to Be True?
Miracle memory drugs, amazing weight loss programs, get rich quick schemes. They all sound too good to be true. Are they? Put your critical thinking skills to the test in working through this activity about memory drugs.

Caveat Emptor: Evaluating Knowledge Claims
Explore how you can become a good consumer of information. Learn how to evaluate the critical features of knowledge claims that you see in advertising or on the Internet.

Searching the Web: Investigating Alzheimer's Disease
How can you make the most of your research time on the World Wide Web? Explore current research on Alzheimer's disease AND learn important Web searching and evaluation skills. With step-by-step instructions, this activity provides interactive assessment exercises on identifying research questions, exploring search methods, and evaluating Web resources.

Research News

Animal Rights Activists: Changing Views on Animal Research
A newly published survey and analysis shows that animal rights activists have shifted some of their views over the past decade. A 1990 survey by psychologist Scott Plous of Wesleyan University revealed that the activists' primary concern was the use of animals in research. A 1996 survey Plous is now reporting shows that while activists still view research animals as an important issue, they have become more concerned about animal agriculture. The newer survey also indicates that activists may now be more willing to discuss their concerns directly with animal researchers instead of engaging in extreme tactics.

Drawing Conclusions: The Child Sexual Abuse Controversy
An article in an American Psychological Association publication suggested that child sexual abuse might not be as harmful as most people assume. A flood of criticism followed. What should we do when we don't like the conclusions scientists draw from data?

Is Embarrassment a Distinct Emotion?
What does it take before psychologists will classify a particular feeling as a distinct emotion? In much of their research on emotions, investigators have overlooked the topic of embarrassment. One research team, however, has recently ventured into this issue and concluded that the feeling is unique and definable.

Op Ed Essays

What Questions are on Psychologists' Minds Today? by David G. Myers, Hope College
What questions are currently driving psychology's most fertile minds? We asked the most oft-cited psychologists in introductory psychology texts and the APA Distinguished Scientific Contribution Award winners from the last decade to tell us, "What is the question you are asking yourself—the question that most fascinates you right now?" Here are their answers.

How Did Leading Psychologists Find Psychology? by David G. Myers, Hope College
Why did some of today's leading psychologists enter the field of psychology? We asked the most-often cited psychologists in introductory psychology texts and APA Distinguished Scientific Contribution Award winners from the last decade to tell us their stories. Read the personal narratives of Phil Zimbardo, Elizabeth Loftus, Eliot Aronson—to name just a few.

Building a Prototype of Master Teaching: Finding Common Ground
What are the characteristics of a master teacher? Explore the views of Bill Buskist and Jane Halonen in the Op Ed Forum.

Building Partnerships in Psychology to Enhance Teaching and Learning
Virginia Andreoli Mathie describes the Psychology Partnerships Project (P3), an initiative of the American Psychological Association. Explore the benefits of partnerships, find out how you can participate in a partnership, and post your ideas for building psychology partnerships in the 21st century.

What are the Implications of National Standards for Teaching Psychology?
Ken Weaver identifies some of the issues and potential pitfalls of setting national standards for teaching high school psychology and invites you to post your views on the issue in the forum.

Ask Dr. Mike

- What's the difference between a psychologist and a psychiatrist?
- What are psychologists most interested in regarding behavior?
- Do I need to go to medical school for a career in research psychology?
- I'm confused about independent and dependent variables. Can you help?
- In order to go to graduate school in psychology, do I need to get a B.A. or a B.S.?
- In the Milgram experiment, why didn't the participants just leave? Aren't you free to leave a study at any time?
- Is it true that Freud was addicted to cocaine?
- My textbook seems to have a LOT of information. How do I know what's important?
- What does $p < .05$ mean? Please help!
- What is a "placebo"?
- What is APA style? Can you give some examples?
- What is factor analysis? I'm lost!
- What kind of grades do you need in high school to be a psychologist, and what classes should you take?
- What's the difference between a random sample and random assignment?
- When writing in APA style, is it okay to put a running head in question form?
- Who is the most "famous" psychologist?

Chapter 2
Biological Foundations of Psychology

Learning Activities

Action at the Synapse
The synapse is where it's at, if you're a neuron communicating with other neurons in the brain. This highly animated, four-part activity focuses on the action at the synapse and some behavioral effects of what happens at the synapse. It includes some review of the action potential, but the emphasis here is on synaptic communication, neurotransmitter effects, and drug effects.

Investigating the Evolutionary Perspective: 3 Dads and a Baby
Do babies resemble their fathers more than they resemble other men? Participate in this online experiment and explore the evolutionary perspective on babies' resemblance to their parents. Is he a "chip off the old block"?

Scientific American Connection

Aging Brain, Aging Mind
Is cognitive decline inevitable as we get older? Later in life the human brain suffers attrition of certain neurons and undergoes chemical alterations. Yet for many people, these changes do not add up to a noticeable decline in intelligence.

Sex Differences in the Brain (1966)
There is increasing evidence that mammalian behavior patterns are basically female and that male patterns are induced by the action of the sex hormone testosterone on the brain of the newborn animal.

Sex Differences in the Brain (1992)
Cognitive variations between the sexes reflect differing hormonal influences on brain development. Understanding these differences and their causes can yield insights into brain organization.

Research News

Second Languages and the Brain: New Organization for Later Learners
Adults who learned two languages during early childhood have a brain organization that differs significantly from those who learned a second language during adolescence. A recent study by a brain-imaging team in New York provides the first direct evidence that in bilingual people, the age at which a second language is acquired influences the physical development of a major language center in the brain.

Cockroach Pheromones Can Cause Social Dominance
The male lobster cockroach has a secret chemical weapon—a pheromone that attracts females and allows them to tell one male from the next. New experiments reveal that variations in the levels of these chemicals actually cause (rather than simply reflect) a male's dominance status in bouts of male-male competition. Additional studies show that a male's environment helps determine the chemical make-up of his alluring odor. This is a striking example of how environmental factors can affect an organism's physiology, and how the physical functioning, in turn, can influence an animal's social behavior.

Sex Alters the Brain
We know that the brain powerfully shapes our behavior, but can behavior also affect the anatomy of the brain? For some time, researchers have known that experience alters brain structure, but now a

45

California neuroscientist has found evidence that engaging in a particular form of behavior can greatly alter the anatomy of individual neurons. Specifically, male rats that engaged in copulatory behavior experience a shrinking in the size of neurons in a specific brain area. These findings may have important implications for the study of human sexuality.

Prenatal Experience: More is Not Better
Experience begins prenatally. Researchers have been studying the effects of normal prenatal experience on development for some time and it is clear that insufficient amounts of embryonic experience can have devastating effects postnatally. A new study of precocial species shows that extra prenatal auditory experience can dramatically alter not only postnatal auditory and visual perception but mortality as well.

Evolutionary Change Before Your Eyes
Lizards that were introduced to new habitats containing shorter, thinner vegetation than that found at their original home evolved shorter hind limbs within 10 years. This study is a remarkable demonstration of the speed and extent of the effects of natural selection under conditions requiring adaptation to dramatic environmental change.

Planum Temporale: Brain Structure Behind Language Evolution?
The planum temporale (PT) region of the human brain is associated with language. This area is the brain's most lateralized anatomical structure, meaning that it is much larger in the left hemisphere than in the right. Until now, anatomists believed that humans were unique with regard to this region's asymmetry. However, a recent study reveals that our closest nonhuman relative, the chimpanzee, also shares asymmetry of the planum temporale. Although researchers don't yet know the function of PT asymmetry in the chimpanzee, this anatomical discovery provides new hypotheses regarding the evolution of human language.

Brain Area Represents Local Visual Environments
Researchers have identified a small portion of the human brain called the "parahippocampal place area" (PPA)—a region that becomes selectively active when we view a local environmental space, such as a room. Through an intriguing series of experiments, researchers demonstrated how the PPA is involved in visual perception by rearranging objects and components of local visual environments. They think the PPA may encode visual memories of the settings we encounter and thereby assist our ability to navigate in local environments.

How the Brain "Hears" Sign Language
How does the brain function when a person is denied input from a major sensory modality? What if that input happens to be spoken language, and what if speech is replaced by a different form of language in an entirely different sensory modality, namely vision? A new study shows that certain areas of the brain that typically respond to spoken language are activated in congenitally deaf people who communicate with sign language. Thus, the language area of the brain functions regardless of whether language is in the form of auditory speech or visual signals.

Adult Brains Can Generate New Neurons
Technological advances have allowed researchers to discover newly formed neurons in the most complex areas of the primate neocortex. The discovery is likely to lead in two exciting directions of research: Scientists are apt to search for a special role new neurons may play in human cognition. They are also likely to explore techniques for increasing the development of new neurons, which might prove useful in promoting recovery from brain damage.

Early Pain Influences the Development of the Nervous System
A recent study of a rat model of infant pain shows that painful stimuli delivered to newborn rats increase the development of neural pain circuits. These results provide strong reasons to aggressively manage pain in infants.

Glia: The Forgotten Majority
Glial cells greatly outnumber neurons in the brain. Until recently, researchers assumed that the function of glial cells was to support neurons in various ways. This view of glial function is now changing with recent discoveries that glial cells play key roles in nervous system function.

Leptin: Weight Loss Panacea or Pipe Dream?
Obesity is a health-threatening crisis of epidemic proportions in the U.S. and other countries around the world in which people consume large amounts of fast foods. The hormone leptin may provide a promising treatment for obesity by signaling the body to reduce fat accumulation. Although the media reported that a recent large-scale clinical trial of leptin confirmed its promise, a closer reading of the study reveals problems.

Pavlovian Conditioning and Meals
Most people tend to think that we are motivated to eat meals by energy deficits. This notion is wrong according to new theoretical insights based on the principles of classical conditioning.

Seeing with Your Auditory Cortex
Modern brain imaging techniques reveal that areas of the human cortex typically activated during auditory speech perception are also activated during the visual component of auditory communications—lipreading. This is of particular interest because lipreading can greatly affect one's ability to perceive speech accurately.

Steroids Elicit Manic Symptoms
Recent experiments confirm that anabolic androgenic steroids provoke aggression and other manic symptoms. These studies almost certainly underestimate the magnitude of the problem because none of them assess the impact of using high doses of combinations of potent steroids taken continually for long periods, conditions commonly experienced by steroid abusers.

Superman, Spinal Damage, and Stem Cell
New research with embryonic neural stem cells may produce a major therapeutic breakthrough in the treatment of spinal cord injuries. Rats with severely damaged spines who received injections with neural stem cells experienced growth of new neurons and glial cells at the site of the damage and eventually gained some control over their hind legs. Although these results are promising, we still need to know more about the factors that direct the course of stem cell development before the therapy can be used on human patients with spinal injury.

The Shape of Beauty: In the Eye of the Beholder?
New research shows that body mass index (BMI)—a ratio of weight scaled for height—is particularly important in mate selection. Moreover, the range of BMIs that males find attractive happens to be the same range that reflects optimal female health and fertility.

Op-Ed Essays

The Mathematics of Beauty
When you are attracted to someone, is a mathematical ratio at the root of your attraction? Find out in The Mathematics of Beauty, by Kristin Saunders, our first STUDENT Op Ed author!

Ask Dr. Mike

- Does the research on "split-brain" patients suggest a basis for the unconscious? Is the left hemisphere conscious, while the right is unconscious?

- What is the cause of ambidexterity?
- What is an antihistamine and how does it work?
- What if a neuron doesn't have enough "firing power?"
- What does all of this physiological stuff have to do with psychology?
- Brain tumor? What are some of the side effects? And if you have surgery, what are the chances of not having anything wrong with that person?
- What's the difference between an action potential and a graded potential?
- What is actually measured when someone measures your "arousal level?"
- Are couples who have twins more likely to have twins again?
- Are there any differences between the male and female brain?
- Can the smaller Y chromosome be considered genetically "inferior" to the larger X chromosome?
- I've heard people use the term "crackpot" for someone who was crazy. Where does this term come from?
- I've heard that Prozac has few, if any, side effects. Is this true?
- If eye color is the result of a dominant (brown) allele and a recessive (blue) allele, how can you have green eyes? Using a Mendel table, the color should be either brown or blue, shouldn't it?
- If the neurotransmitter serotonin enhances mood, how is it related to depression?
- Is alcoholism genetic?
- Is it true that people with PKU can't drink milk?
- Is lithium the only drug treatment for bipolar disorder?
- Is there a chemical in turkey that makes you sleepy?
- Is there a greater tendency for homosexuals to be left-handed?
- What are the effects of PCP on the brain?
- What are the major neurotransmitters and their functions?
- What do you think may be the next most important discovery about the brain?
- What does the spleen do?
- What is a "split-brain" procedure?
- What is a migraine headache?
- What is dysgraphia?
- What is serotonin?
- What is THC and how does it work?
- Why does psychology favor Darwin's theory of evolution over creationism?

Chapter Three
Sensation and Perception

Learning Activities

Investigating Depth Perception
When looking at a painting, why do we perceive some parts of it as farther away than others? The eye's retina, like a painting or a photograph, is two-dimensional, so how do we perceive the world in three dimensions? In this activity, you will explore how the brain interprets different depth cues in order to accurately perceive the three-dimensional world. Test your own accuracy in perceiving the depth of objects, and compare your responses with those of fellow students.

Investigating Olfaction: The Nose Knows
Are you aware of the powerful influence of olfaction, your sense of smell, in your daily life? How does the olfactory system work? This highly interactive learning activity investigates olfaction and how it influences human behavior.

Research News

Seeing with Your Auditory Cortex
Modern brain imaging techniques reveal that areas of the human cortex typically activated during auditory speech perception are also activated during the visual component of auditory communications—lipreading. This is of particular interest because lipreading can greatly affect one's ability to perceive speech accurately.

Brain Area Represents Local Visual Environments
Researchers have identified a small portion of the human brain called the "parahippocampal place area" (PPA)—a region that becomes selectively active when we view a local environmental space, such as a room. Through an intriguing series of experiments, researchers demonstrated how the PPA is involved in visual perception by rearranging objects and components of local visual environments. They think the PPA may encode visual memories of the settings we encounter and thereby assist our ability to navigate in local environments.

Auditory Perceptual Deficits in Language-Impaired Children
Children affected with Specific Language Impairment (SLI) have severe language deficits but otherwise are intellectually normal. Psychophysical experiments now reveal that SLI children differ from normal children in the way they detect speechlike sounds. This altered form of auditory perception may play a role in the altered form of speech production characteristic of SLI children.

Ask Dr. Mike

- How do you explain those "magic eye 3D pictures?"
- What happens when your eye becomes "bloodshot?"
- Are carrots good for your eyesight?
- Do cartoons appear to move through the autokinetic effect?
- Young infants seem to show a preference for looking at faces. Could this be due to the fact that faces are the only things they've seen in the delivery room?
- When older people begin to have problems with their vision, does this have anything to do with damage to the visual cortex?
- Can you explain Fechner's Law?
- Does time really go faster as you get older?
- How can we perceive dreams as visual images since we sleep with eyes closed and the receptors are not firing?
- How does acupuncture work?
- How would a behaviorist explain the operation of an aphrodisiac?
- I know that the moon can't really be bigger when it's just rising, but it looks that way. Why?
- I'm always confused by the terms "nearsighted" and "farsighted." In which is your vision good for close objects?
- Is sense of smell different in females and males?
- What actually happens during laser eye surgery?
- What causes dyslexia?
- What is synesthesia?

- What is THC and how does it work?
- What is the visual system, what is color vision, and what are the differences in color vision among different species? And what does any of this have to do with psychology?
- Why can you sometimes still see flashing lights or "spots" after you shut your eyes?
- Why do we see impossible images?
- Why do you sometimes feel that the eyes of a person in a painting are "following" you?
- Why do your ears get "blocked" and "pop" when landing in an airplane?

Chapter Four
Motivation and Emotion

Learning Activities

Exploring Academic Dishonesty
Academic dishonesty, or cheating, is not uncommon in today's colleges and universities. But when does cheating begin? What motivates students to cheat? And can anything be done to stop it? Learn more about the issues and research regarding this highly publicized topic and do your own research using the activities provided.

Scientific American Connection

Emotion, Memory and the Brain
A sight, a smell or a chord from a melody can evoke an emotional memory. How does the brain recall such emotions? Experiments with rodents model the process. Nerve impulses from sounds that cause fear in rats have been traced along the auditory pathway to the thalamus, the cortex and the amygdala, arousing a memory that leads to a higher heart rate and the cessation of movement.

Research News

Is Embarrassment a Distinct Emotion?
What does it take before psychologists will classify a particular feeling as a distinct emotion? In much of their research on emotions, investigators have overlooked the topic of embarrassment. One research team, however, has recently ventured into this issue and concluded that the feeling is unique and definable.

Should Creativity Be Rewarded?
Both folk wisdom and past psychological studies warn parents and educators to avoid the dangers of overusing rewards. Observers, from the casual to the scientific, have suggested that rewarding creativity on a task reduces intrinsic interest and further creativity on that and future tasks. A theory put forth by Robert Eisenberger of the University of Delaware, however, and a new study by him and two colleagues suggests a very different point of view.

Giving Children Rewards: A Right Way and a Wrong Way
Using prizes, such as stars or money, to reward academic effort may not necessarily be as bad as some critics suggest. Indeed, recent research suggests that misuse of rewards may be responsible for the reduction in children's creativity and intrinsic motivation observed in earlier studies. Verbal praise given for effort, rather than for ability, is suggested as the best motivator.

Ask Dr. Mike

- When I get angry, why does my chest start to hurt?
- What is a "lie detector?"
- Do animals imitate? If so, what does this mean?
- Can a polygraph really determine whether or not you're lying? How could I do a demonstration on lying in the classroom?
- Does alcohol really kill brain cells?
- How would a behaviorist explain the operation of an aphrodisiac?
- I have been on Prozac for about 6 to 8 months now, and I have been having very violent and disturbing dreams. Could this be a side effect of the Prozac?
- Is catharsis a good thing or a bad thing? I've heard both.
- Is there any evidence to suggest that homosexuality is due to "nature" rather than "nurture"?
- My friend and I have bet and hope you can settle it for us. Who is better at lying, men or women?
- What can you tell me about Rohypnol?
- What is actually measured when someone measures your "arousal level"?
- What is emotional intelligence? Is it the same thing as IQ?
- What is narcolepsy? And can narcolepsy affect your sex life?
- Why do people yawn?
- Why does a moth fly toward a light?
- Why is it that sometimes people think you're lying when you're not lying at all?

Chapter Five
States of Consciousness

Learning Activities

Drug Use, Abuse, and Addictions: Focus on Alcohol
In this activity, you will examine where drug abuse and addictions begin with a special focus on alcohol and its use among young people today. You will engage in a debate on lowering the drinking age and keep track of your own substance use.

Investigating Dreams
Ever wonder about your crazy dreams? Would interpreting your dreams provide you with any special insights? Here's an opportunity to try it yourself and find out. First, review the prevalent dream theories, then, over a three-week period, record and interpret your own dreams. All the materials you'll need are provided here.

Research News

Cigarette Smoking and Genetics: A Not So Unlikely Combination (3/29/98)
Why is it easy for some people to quit smoking, while others can't seem to kick the habit? Why do some people start smoking in the first place? New research suggests that part of the answer to these questions may lie in the presence or absence of specific genes. More information about genes identified with smoking risk can ultimately identify who is at risk for nicotine dependence and can help determine the best way to quit smoking.

One Eye Open: How Sleeping Ducks Avoid Becoming "Sitting Ducks"

How do you protect yourself from intruders when you're asleep? You probably depend on mechanical means, such as window locks, deadbolts, and alarm systems. Nonhuman organisms, however, can't go to the hardware store for help. They must rely on natural strategies to protect themselves from predators. Recently, researchers discovered a remarkable strategy used by mallard ducks: By sleeping with one eye open and one eye shut, they can keep one brain hemisphere in a sleep state and the other awake and alert for danger. This discovery has some interesting implications for the relationship between brain and behavior.

Psychoactive Drugs for Children: Panacea or Peril?

Over three million children in the United States are currently taking Ritalin, more than double the number in 1990. An additional estimated 580,000 children are currently being prescribed antidepressants. With more than 4 four million children taking powerful drugs to manage their behavior, a major controversy is brewing among professionals concerned with the health and welfare of children.

Scientists Battle Nicotine

Two new drugs, NicVAX and methoxsalen, appear to have potential in the treatment of chronic smoking. Paradoxically, although both drugs are hypothesized to reduce the craving for nicotine, they have opposite effects on nicotine levels in the brain. NicVAX reduces them, and methoxsalen increases them.

The Secret to Better Grades Might Be More Sleep

Publicity based on recent research extols the virtue of sleep for learning. Some sleep researchers believe that at least 6 hours of sleep can improve learning and memory. They think the first two and the last two hours of sleep are especially precious for the consolidation of memories. However, not all sleep researchers agree that sleep aids memory and learning.

Op Ed Essays

Are We Chronically Sleep-Deprived? by Stanley Coren

We have heard it, taught it, believed it: We have widely varying sleep needs. We can adapt to less sleep and still function well. In any case, 7 hours is plenty for the average adult.

We have heard, taught, and believed wrongly, argues University of British Columbia neuropsychologist Stanley Coren in his fascinating book *Sleep Thieves* (Free Press, 1996). Evidence ranging from unrestricted sleep length to Canadian traffic accident rates on the day following "Spring forward" drives him to a surprising conclusion: We are biologically prepared for more sleep than we're getting.

A Harmful Psychoactive Drug for Children

Andrea and Sarah, winners of the Student Op Ed contest, presented some excellent views on the use and possible abuse of Ritalin. We encourage students and faculty to join in a discussion of this timely and hotly debated topic. How do your views compare to those of Andrea, Sarah, and Dr. Christine Ziegler? Have they overlooked any issue?

Scientific American Connection

The Meaning of Dreams by Jonathan Winson (1998)

What are we to make of all our bizarre dreams? Are they merely our brain's best attempt to make sense of random neural firing, as physiological theories have proposed? Or was Freud right that dreams are the "royal road to our unconscious?" Researcher Jonathan Winson has deftly combined elements of those and other theories with his own work to create a clearer explanation of the meaning of our dreams. (See related activity)

Ask Dr. Mike

- What is THC and how does it work?
- Is it possible to walk or act out behavior while dreaming?
- If you dream that you are falling and if you hit the ground, will you die?
- Can dreams predict the future? How do you explain the fact that sometimes you dream about something and then it happens?
- How do you figure out that a particular symbol stands for something else in a dream?
- We have been talking a lot in class about ESP. What is your opinion on this subject?
- Are dreams and visions something to worry about? Do they affect our lives in any way?
- Can learning occur "unconsciously" as suggested in "learn while you sleep" tapes?
- Can reinforcement be presented "subconsciously"? Can we learn without being aware?
- Can we control our dreams?
- Can you become addicted to the Internet?
- Can you practice to have a lucid dream? How?
- Do people in comas dream?
- Does everyone dream? If not, why?
- How do you figure out that a particular symbol stands for something else in a dream?
- If a person snores, does this mean that they have a mild case of sleep apnea?
- Is alcoholism genetic?
- Is there a chemical in turkey that makes you sleepy?
- I've heard that Seasonal Affective Disorder (SAD) is caused by a lack of sunlight, but is it also related to temperature?
- My textbook says that serotonin is an inhibitory neurotransmitter. It also says that LSD blocks serotonin receptor sites, implying that LSD is an antagonist (as the inhibitory effects of serotonin are blocked). Yet in the Psychology Place, Kolb and Wishaw (1996) are cited as describing LSD as an agonist. What is LSD, agonist or antagonist, and why?
- We have been talking a lot in class about ESP. What is your opinion on this subject?
- What are the effects of PCP on the brain?
- What are the long-term risks of taking the drug Adderall?
- What can you tell me about Rohypnol?
- What can you tell me about the drug, "ecstasy"?
- What is narcolepsy? And can narcolepsy affect your sex life?
- Why do people yawn?

Chapter Six
Basic Principles of Learning

Learning Activities

Principles of Learning in the Real World
What do salivating dogs, pecking pigeons, and bar-pressing rats have to do with real life? In this activity, you will see the key processes in classical conditioning, operant conditioning, and observational learning in action. By interacting with our dog, Buster and our rat, Dexter, you experience the development of a conditioned response and the paradigms for reinforcement and punishment.

Research News

Songbird Brain Cell Count Predicts Learning
Do the numbers of neurons in certain areas of your brain limit how much you are capable of learning? The answer appears to be "yes"—as long as you're a zebra finch. Researchers have found a strong relationship between the number of neurons in one song-production nucleus of the zebra finch brain and the number of song syllables the birds actually learned from social tutors. The neural numbers did not, however, relate to the entire repertoire of all zebra finch songs. This represents a remarkably specific relationship between neuron number and learning rather than instinctive song production in general.

Giving Children Rewards: A Right Way and a Wrong Way
Using prizes, such as stars or money, to reward academic effort may not necessarily be as bad as some critics suggest. Indeed, recent research suggests that misuse of rewards may be responsible for the reduction in children's creativity and intrinsic motivation observed in earlier studies. Verbal praise given for effort, rather than for ability, is suggested as the best motivator.

Beyond Pavlov's Dogs
Pavlov's principles of conditioning apply to more than salivating dogs. Recent studies by three research groups demonstrates the importance of Pavlovian conditioning in a wide range of behaviors, such as defense, mating and reproduction, immune system suppression, drug tolerance and addiction.

Should Creativity Be Rewarded?
Both folk wisdom and past psychological studies warn parents and educators to avoid the dangers of overusing rewards. Observers, from the casual to the scientific, have suggested that rewarding creativity on a task reduces intrinsic interest and further creativity on that and future tasks. A theory put forth by Robert Eisenberger of the University of Delaware, however, and a new study by him and two colleagues suggests a very different point of view.

Numerical Ability in Chimpanzees
Researchers are still hotly debating whether nonhuman animals are capable of symbolic representation with a richness even approaching our own abilities. Language is an obvious example of such symbol use, but the jury is still out on true language capacity in other animals. In the meantime, Sarah Boysen and her colleagues have published new research exploring the numerical representation skills of chimpanzees. While they may not be functionally equivalent to our own counting and numbering talents, they do provide a fascinating glimpse into the primate mind.

Pavlovian Conditioning and Meals
Most people tend to think that we are motivated to eat meals by energy deficits. This notion is wrong according to new theoretical insights based on the principles of classical conditioning.

Ask Dr. Mike

- If you punish a response (e.g., bar pressing), what happens when you no longer deliver the punishment?
- In a counterconditioning procedure, can you get a transfer of fear to the positive stimulus rather than the other way around?
- Can reinforcement be presented "unconsciously?" Can we learn without being aware?
- My students have a tough time in distinguishing between negative reinforcement and punishment. What are some good examples of each?
- In Pavlov's studies, wouldn't he have trouble controlling the dogs as soon as they entered the experimental room? Wouldn't they learn to salivate at the sight and sound of the door?
- How would a behaviorist explain the operation of an aphrodisiac?

- I've heard that aluminum may cause Alzheimer's Disease. Should I worry about drinking from aluminum cans?
- My dog has severe reactions to thunderstorms. He shakes, pants, and appears to be in a state of panic. Lately he reacts the same way to cars, trucks, and even rain on the roof. The vet prescribed an antianxiety medicine, but is there a nonmedical way to treat my dog?
- What's the difference between desensitization, counterconditioning, and aversive conditioning?
- When a person develops a taste aversion but doesn't remember the incident surrounding the aversion, how is this explained in terms of classical conditioning?

Chapter Seven
Memory

Learning Activities

Product Claims: Too Good to Be True?
Miracle memory drugs, amazing weight loss programs, get rich quick schemes. They all sound too good to be true. Are they? Put your critical thinking skills to the test in working through this activity about memory drugs.

Test Your Memory
Here's your chance to test your own memory. You will play the role of an observer—an eyewitness—who is present when an embarrassing event occurs. After you observe the event, you will be asked some questions about what you remember about the event. After completing this activity, you will want to read the article by Elizabeth Loftus.

Research News

The Repressed Memory Debate
For years, a contentious debate has raged over adults' recovered memories of child abuse. Psychologists on both sides of the debate have used the American Psychological Association's conventions and publications as forums. Increasingly, the arguments are spilling over into the World Wide Web and, in some cases, have taken on a vitriolic tone. This article summarizes issues on each side to help readers think critically about the positions.

Another Measure of Intelligence: Working Memory
Researchers are finding that working memory is a good predictor of verbal and non-verbal problem solving. Recent studies measuring working memory were highly correlated with scores on the verbal SAT, the Raven's Progressive Matrices test, and other tests.

The Secret to Better Grades Might Be More Sleep
Publicity based on recent research extols the virtue of sleep for learning. Some sleep researchers believe that at least 6 hours of sleep can improve learning and memory. They think the first two and the last two hours of sleep are especially precious for the consolidation of memories. However, not all sleep researchers agree that sleep aids memory and learning.

Op Ed Essays

Recovered-memory Experiences: Explaining True and False Delayed Memories of Childhood Sexual Abuse by D. Stephen Lindsay

No issue in psychology has aroused as much passion during the 1990s as claims that people, sometimes aided by therapists, have recovered long-repressed memory of horrific child abuse. Critics have responded that such memories often are recovered under conditions known to produce false memories. So who is right? Are clinicians who use "memory work" techniques "merchants of mental chaos" and a blight on the profession of psychology? Or are critics who dispute the accuracy of recovered memories playing into the hands of child molesters?

The Psychology Place explores this issue with a Scientific American Connection that builds on an article by American Psychological Society president, Elizabeth Loftus, and with this helpful essay by memory researcher Stephen Lindsay, who draws on his dozen years of pertinent research, his many writings, and his conversations with people on both sides.

Scientific American Connection

Creating False Memories by Elizabeth Loftus (1997)
Researchers are showing how suggestion and imagination can create "memories" of events that did not actually occur. (See related activity)

Emotion, Memory, and the Brain by Joseph E. LeDoux (1994)
A sight, a smell, or a chord from a melody can evoke an emotional memory. How does the brain recall such emotions? Experiments with rodents model the process. Nerve impulses from sounds that cause fear in rats have been traced along the auditory pathway to the thalamus, the cortex, and the amygdala, arousing a memory that leads to a higher heart rate and the cessation of movement.

Ask Dr. Mike

- If the proper cue could be found, would it be possible to retrieve any memory?
- Is any particular type of music related to memory recall in positive or negative ways? How and why?
- Can the environmental context influence memory?
- Does dementia lead to Alzheimer's disease or is it a separate disorder?
- Is there a way to measure a person's memory span?
- Since we can get primacy and recency effects for memory, does this mean that it is better to study in smaller chunks, taking breaks?
- What is Ginkgo? Does it improve memory?
- What is synesthesia?

Chapter Eight
Thinking and Intelligence

Learning Activities

Understanding Mental Models
Why are there 24 hours in a day? Is broccoli or a chocolate bar healthier food? The answers you give to these questions depend on how you process abstract concepts. Discover how faulty mental processing or mental models work by participating in interactive demonstrations.

Critical Thinking: I Know It's a Good Thing, but What Is It?
This tutorial will help you to review the processes of critical thinking. Examine a few scenarios and test your ability to recognize critical thinking in action.

Making Sound Decisions: The Worksheet Method
In this activity, we present a technique to use when facing life's difficult and important decisions. Using a decision-making worksheet developed by Diane Halpern, you will learn to make better decisions.

Product Claims: Too Good to be True?
Miracle memory drugs, amazing weight loss programs, get rich quick schemes. They all sound too good to be true. Are they? Put your critical thinking skills to the test in working through this activity about memory drugs.

Research News

The Growing Popularity of "Emotional Intelligence"
The release of Daniel Goleman's best-selling book *Emotional Intelligence* was one of the top publishing events of 1995, and garnered a giant following for Goleman's argument that emotional intelligence (EQ) can matter more than IQ. Since then, the subject has inspired numerous articles in popular magazines as well as a plethora of websites. When it comes to those spin-offs, buyers beware! Media and Internet writers are claiming—with little or no research support—that EQ can be taught, is the truest measure of human intelligence, is necessary for some career success, and is related to success in life.

Auditory Perceptual Deficits in Language-Impaired Children
Children affected with Specific Language Impairment (SLI) have severe language deficits but otherwise are intellectually normal. Psychophysical experiments now reveal that SLI children differ from normal children in the way they detect speechlike sounds. This altered form of auditory perception may play a role in the altered form of speech production characteristic of SLI children.

Planum Temporale: Brain Structure Behind Language Evolution?
The planum temporale (PT) region of the human brain is associated with language. This area is the brain's most lateralized anatomical structure, meaning that it is much larger in the left hemisphere than in the right. Until now, anatomists believed that humans were unique with regard to this region's asymmetry. However, a recent study reveals that our closest nonhuman relative, the chimpanzee, also shares asymmetry of the planum temporale. Although researchers don't yet know the function of PT asymmetry in the chimpanzee, this anatomical discovery provides new hypotheses regarding the evolution of human language.

Another Explanation for Differences in Intellectual Performance: Stereotype Threat
Claude Steele (1997) suggests that negative stereotypes about women and African Americans may impair their performance in the classroom and on standardized tests. Steele also suggests that stereotype threat may be responsible for underperformance in the classroom by students from these same two groups. Additionally, he suggests that stereotyped groups may use disidentification, which serves to protect their self-esteem.

How the Brain "Hears" Sign Language
How does the brain function when a person is denied input from a major sensory modality? What if that input happens to be spoken language, and what if speech is replaced by a different form of language in an entirely different sensory modality, namely vision? A new study shows that certain areas of the brain that typically respond to spoken language are activated in congenitally deaf people who communicate

with sign language. Thus, the language area of the brain functions regardless of whether language is in the form of auditory speech or visual signals.

Babies, Phonetics, and Mastering Language
Babies and young children are masters of language acquisition. What's behind the innate human ability to learn the sounds and meanings of spoken words in infancy, then to communicate back with increasing fluency? New research details the roles of "parentese" and "phonetic screening," and may help guide the teaching of second languages to teens and adults.

Second Languages and the Brain: New Organization for Later Learners
Adults who learned two languages during early childhood have a brain organization that differs significantly from those who learned a second language during adolescence. A recent study by a brain-imaging team in New York provides the first direct evidence that in bilingual people, the age at which a second language is acquired influences the physical development of a major language center in the brain.

Another Measure of Intelligence: Working Memory
Researchers are finding that working memory is a good predictor of verbal and non-verbal problem solving. Recent studies measuring working memory were highly correlated with scores on the verbal SAT, the Raven's Progressive Matrices test, and other tests.

How Stereotypes Affect Test Performance
Women are generally considered to be "not so good in math," while men are generally supposed to be "good in math." But is it true? Recent research shows that both negative and positive stereotypes about math ability may affect the performance of men and women on math tests.

Ask Dr. Mike

- What is the "Chitterling Test?"
- What causes dyslexia?
- What is Savant Syndrome and what causes it?
- If savants are so good at counting, why can't they make change for $1.00?
- Can your IQ level change over time?
- Is the term "mentally retarded" still acceptable?
- Are there really racial differences in intelligence?
- Can you explain cognition in a manner that a child would understand?
- Does group size affect the quality of decision making? If smaller groups make better decisions, why do we have juries composed of 12 people?
- How can I tell how many morphemes there are in a word?
- If you administered both the Stanford-Binet test and the WISC test to the same person, would you derive the same IQ score?
- Is it true that playing music to a baby while it is still in the womb can increase the child's intelligence?
- Should the Stanford-Binet scale be changed over time since children's abilities are probably changing?
- What does a score of 90 on an IQ test mean?
- What is dysgraphia?
- What is the distinction between Thurstone's theory of intelligence and that offered by Sternberg?
- Why do child prodigies, or highly gifted children, burn out so quickly or never really make it in the real world?

Chapter Nine
Developmental Psychology I

Learning Activities

Tick Tock Goes the Social and Biological Clock
Our bodies pull us in some ways; our cultures pull us in others. What are the relative effects of each, how do they interact, how are they changing? Play the Longevity Game and find out how your calculated life expectancy affects your social clock.

Investigating the Evolutionary Perspective: 3 Dads and a Baby
Do babies resemble their fathers more than they resemble other men? Participate in this online experiment and explore the evolutionary perspective on babies' resemblance to their parents. Is he a "chip off the old block"?

Research News

Daycare: What's a Parent to Do?
Virtually all working parents struggle with questions about daycare. When parents who must work have no other options, daycare is inevitable. Still, they worry about how long periods of time in another's care will affect their children. Research done in the 1980s indicated that extended daycare could be detrimental to the mother-child relationship, or produce more aggressive and noncompliant children. A series of recent studies, however, has changed that picture.

Nature vs. Nurture: Genes Win Again!
One of the longest running debates in psychology is the so-called "nature versus nurture" controversy: Is heredity or environment the primary determinant of human potential?

Birth Month Predicts Height?
A 10-year study of more than half a million males has revealed a reliable, cyclic relationship between birth month and height at age 18. The cyclicity of the height/birth month relationship trails sunshine duration by about three months: As the duration of sunshine increases, so does height, but three months later. The authors of a new paper on this phenomenon speculate that the height/birth month relationship may involve the light-sensitive hormone melatonin and its influence on the rapidly growing fetus and very young infant.

Babies, Phonetics, and Mastering Language
Babies and young children are masters of language acquisition. What's behind the innate human ability to learn the sounds and meanings of spoken words in infancy, then to communicate back with increasing fluency? New research details the roles of "parentese" and "phonetic screening," and may help guide the teaching of second languages to teens and adults.

Infant Attachment, Adult Curiosity, and Cognitive Closure
Recent research has explored the relationship between people's early emotional attachments and their approach to information processing later in life. Individuals who had experienced secure relationships as infants were found to be more open to new experiences and new information than individuals who had less secure early relationships.

Childhood Attachment Style: How Stable Over the Life Span?
Attachment—the bond between parent and child—forms in infancy and continues into adulthood. Most research on attachment in adults assumes that the quality of early attachment (secure, avoidant, or

ambivalent) remains relatively stable throughout the life span. But is this premise correct? A new report by Joanne Davila and coworkers at U.C.L.A. suggests that approximately 30 percent of the population change their attachment in adulthood. They found that those prone to fluctuations in adulthood tended to have insecure attachments to parents early in life. The researchers also found among the fluctuators more frequent histories of personal and family psychopathology, higher levels of personality disturbance, and a greater chance of having divorced, separated, or deceased parents.

Should Parents Intervene in Children's Fights?
When it comes to their children's conflicts, parents face tough questions. While childcare specialists continue to debate the pros and cons of intervening, parents must decide on a daily basis whether to break up fights and how to do it fairly and wisely. A new study by Canadian researchers documented the fighting behaviors of 2- and 4-year-old children and the effects of both parental action and nonaction. Intervention, the researchers found, seemed to decrease the intensity of conflicts, while providing parents an opportunity to model invaluable conflict resolution skills.

Even Light Maternal Drinking Affects the Unborn Child
Alcohol use by a pregnant women can permanently harm the unborn fetus. Formerly, researchers thought this applied only to heavy drinkers. An accumulation of evidence, however, including some recently published, shows that even light drinking may result in cognitive and behavioral problems that seem not to improve as the child grows older. Fetal alcohol syndrome brought about by heavy drinking is the most common known cause of mental retardation, and yet it is completely preventable.

Attention Deficit Disorder—A Potential Advantage
In the eyes of many critics, school children are too frequently diagnosed with attention deficit hyperactivity disorder and given stimulant drugs to treat it. Recently, however, a number of authors argue that in adulthood ADHD has positive aspects and may be linked to success for some people. Are adults with the disorder merely expressing relief at finally knowing what has been "wrong" all their lives or are researchers overlooking something

Child Development: The Neighborhood Effect
Several recent studies examine the influence of neighborhoods on the development of children. Methodologically, it is difficult to disentangle the causal effects of the neighborhood on child development from hereditary factors. Although these studies suggest that neighborhood environment does affect children, the effect appears to be small.

Drawing Conclusions: The Child Sexual Abuse Controversy
An article in an American Psychological Association publication suggested that child sexual abuse might not be as harmful as most people assume. A flood of criticism followed. What should we do when we don't like the conclusions scientists draw from data?

Is a Male Role Model Essential to Positive Child Development?
Conventional wisdom suggests that a family with a mother and a father is the best model for raising children. Children raised without a male parent are often the target of political attention when these children commit a violent act or crime. Recently, a controversial article challenged the assumption that two-parent, heterosexual families are better than single-parent or gay and lesbian families. Not surprisingly, criticism has been strong.

Nature vs. Nurture: Genes Win Again!
One of the longest running debates in psychology is the so-called "nature versus nurture" controversy: Is heredity or environment the primary determinant of human potential?

Op Ed Essays

Challenging the Nurture Assumption
Judith Rich Harris recants. She "no longer believes" much of what she has taught students through her developmental psychology textbooks. In a recent *Psychological Review* article (that has just been named a winner of APA Division 1's George A. Miller Award for outstanding general psychology article) and in her Free Press book *The Nurture Assumption* Harris asks, "Do parents have any important long-term effects on the development of their child's personality?" After examining the evidence, she concludes "The answer is no." Rather, genes and peer influences shape children. Thus, if we left a group of children with their same schools, neighborhoods, and peers, but switched the parents around, they would, she believes, "develop into the same sort of adults."

The Power of Parents by Jerome Kagan, Harvard University
In *The Nurture Assumption*, Judith Rich Harris argues that peers, not parents, shape children. Jerome Kagan answers Harris's challenge, noting why he believes "parents clearly do matter."

Children's Private Speech: Meaningless Chatter or Essential Tool?
Laura Berk has presented some thought-provoking research results and theory on private speech. How generalizable are these findings? Is Vygotsky's theory correct? How can our current knowledge of private speech help parents' and teachers' interactions with children?

Ask Dr. Mike

- What is a "critical period?"
- If a mother smokes during pregnancy, are there any effects on the fetus?
- Is "Motherese" universal—does this appear in all cultures?
- Do young children have a conscience?
- What are the causes of various attachment styles? Is it the parent's behavior or the child's?
- If eye color is the result of a dominant (brown) allele and a recessive (blue) allele, how can you have green eyes? Using a Mendel table, the color should be either brown or blue, shouldn't it?
- To what extent does the lack of infant attachment adversely influence adult behavior?
- If attachment is strong and secure at an early age, what happens when you move out on your own? Do you have to replace this secure attachment?
- We recently saw the videotape entitled "Secret of the Wild Child." This was a NOVA special featuring the unique story of the young girl who was found in California in the early 1970s after having endured almost total social isolation. My students and I were curious to know where and how Genie is today. Could you tell us what became of her?
- Are couples who have twins more likely to have twins again?
- Can the smaller Y chromosome be considered genetically "inferior" to the larger X chromosome?
- Does violence on TV make children do violent things? Do children get ideas from TV or do they think what they see on TV is real?
- Is TV violence getting worse?
- Is walking at an early age a sign of future athletic ability?
- I've heard that in the first moments of life a baby should be held by its mother in order for bonding to occur. Is this true?
- What's the first word that an infant learns?
- Whom do babies resemble more, their mothers or their fathers? My sister just had a baby boy and he looks exactly like she did in her baby pictures.

Chapter Ten
Developmental Psychology II

Learning Activities

Tick Tock Goes the Social and Biological Clock
Our bodies pull us in some ways; our cultures pull us in others. What are the relative effects of each, how do they interact, how are they changing? Play the Longevity Game and find out how your calculated life expectancy affects your social clock.

Searching the Web: Investigating Alzheimer's Disease
How can you make the most of your research time on the World Wide Web? Explore current research on Alzheimer's disease AND learn important Web searching and evaluation skills. With step-by-step instructions, this activity provides interactive assessment exercises on identifying research questions, exploring search methods, and evaluating Web resources.

Scientific American

Aging Brain, Aging Mind
Is cognitive decline inevitable as we get older? Later in life the human brain suffers attrition of certain neurons and undergoes chemical alterations. Yet for many people, these changes do not add up to a noticeable decline in intelligence.

Research News

Teen Suicide—Symptom of a Changing World or Exaggerated Suggestibility in Adolescence?
Suicide is one of the most frequent causes of death, worldwide, in the adolescent age group. Psychologists have explained this phenomenon in various ways, including despair for the future and an enhanced suggestibility in adolescents. A recent case of six suicides, all by hanging, of young men from the same Boston community seems to illustrate several psychological phenomena.

Fear of Death: Our Final Developmental Crisis
New research headed by psychologists at the University of Arizona lends experimental support to a theory about how people handle the fear of death. The evidence may help explain people's cultural biases toward their "own kind," especially during wartime. And it tends to corroborate Freud's notion that the unconscious mind continues processing information. A self-test lets you measure your own anxiety over death and dying.

Primate Caretakers Live Longer
Overall, the parents in primate species who are invested in doing a good job in raising their young are rewarded evolutionarily by having children who survive to adulthood and possibly continue the gene line. But new research among various primate species, including humans, shows that the parent investing the greater amount of caretaking time gets an added bonus: namely, a longer life span.

Regrets? . . . I've Had a Few: Women's Midlife Review and Well-Being
Until recently, social scientists have tended to view midlife as a developmental stage that requires a major adaptation—especially for women, who must deal with the negative stereotypes associated with aging

women. Contemporary studies have begun to focus on the midlife adaptations of women by examining their regrets about choices in early life, and whether making relevant changes in midlife is related to differences in adjustment.

Sharing Secrets: Siblings and Self-Disclosure
A recent study investigated the ways in which adult brothers and sisters share highly personal and confidential information. It found some essential differences between how we share our secrets with friends and with siblings, and underscored the importance of a good sibling relationship to lifelong support.

Successful Aging: A Matter of Control?
The United States is getting grayer: By the year 2050, according to current projections, the elderly will represent more than 20% of the population. Not surprisingly, researchers are interested in determining which characteristics contribute to a more successful experience with aging. Much of the current research suggests that feeling a sense of control over our lives is an important factor, and one that is strongly affected by our economic status and level of education.

Op Ed Essays

Who or What is to Blame for the Littleton Massacre? by Kevin Byrd, University of Nebraska at Kearney
Is there one single cause for the tragedy at Columbine High School? What do we need to know about our teenagers? Clinical psychologist Kevin Byrd proposes some answers and invites you to post your views on the forum.

Challenging the Nurture Assumption
Judith Rich Harris recants. She "no longer believes" much of what she has taught students through her developmental psychology textbooks. In a recent *Psychological Review* article (that has just been named a winner of APA Division 1's George A. Miller Award for outstanding general psychology article) and in her Free Press book *The Nurture Assumption* Harris asks, "Do parents have any important long-term effects on the development of their child's personality?" After examining the evidence, she concludes "The answer is no." Rather, genes and peer influences shape children. Thus, if we left a group of children with their same schools, neighborhoods, and peers, but switched the parents around, they would, she believes, "develop into the same sort of adults."

The Power of Parents by Jerome Kagan, Harvard University
In *The Nurture Assumption*, Judith Rich Harris argues that peers, not parents, shape children. Jerome Kagan answers Harris's challenge, noting why he believes "parents clearly do matter."

The Tragedy of Adolescent Suicide—Finding Options for Prevention
Suicide is a major cause of death among children and adolescents. Unfortunately, suicide rates for adolescents and young adults are increasing dramatically. What societal factors serve to exacerbate adolescent suicide rates? What individual risk factors are involved? In this Op-Ed feature Barbara Sarason provides illuminating answers to these questions and addresses the challenges of suicide prevention. Her expertise and sensitivity provide an overview and excellent insight into this relevant and disturbing topic.

Scientific American Connection

The Oldest Old by Thomas T. Perls (1998)
People in their late nineties are often healthier and more robust than those 20 years younger. Traditional views of aging may need rethinking. (See related activity)

Ask Dr. Mike

- Did TV violence cause the Littleton situation?
- Does dementia lead to Alzheimer's disease or is it a separate disorder?
- I read an article recently where they said that having a "wet dream" was a normal experience and did not reflect a psychological disorder. Is this true or does it really reflect a disorder?
- Recently, I shared with my AP Psychology class a videotape entitled "Secret of the Wild Child." This was a NOVA special featuring the unique story of the young girl who was found in California in the early 1970s after having endured almost total social isolation. My students and I were curious to know where and how Genie is today. Could you tell us what became of her?

Chapter Eleven
Sex and Gender

Learning Activities

Investigating Sex Differences in Depression
Is there a gender bias in depression? Become a part of an online study and discover the truth. Find out your score on the Self-Rating Depression Scale and compare your results with the study averages for your gender, then see how our results compare to the national averages. After completing this activity, you will want to read the article by Kristin Leutwyler.

Research News

Eating Disorders and Sudden Death
It has been said that a woman can never be too thin or too rich. However, sometimes excessive thinness (or the manner of achieving it) can become a death sentence for women or men. Especially in the worlds of entertainment, modeling, and sports, women often feel pressured to be thin. A recent case shows how this drive for thinness can get out of control, emphasizing the dangerous consequences of eating disorders.

Scent of a Woman: The Scientific Sequel
Many species, including humans, employ pheromones or chemical signals that convey information to and cause specific reactions in other individuals of the same species. Recent experiments have shown that the sex pheromones of female rats in estrus are both necessary and sufficient to elicit a sexual fixed action pattern in male rats, namely, penile erection. This is the first evidence of an airborne pheromone eliciting an instinctive, highly stereotyped behavioral pattern in any mammalian species.

Does Being Female Increase Depression Risks for Females?
Can the way women think affect their tendency to become depressed? Researchers believe that women's ruminative thinking style may be the key to explaining why, from early adolescence on, they are more likely than men to report being depressed or to be diagnosed with depression.

The Shape of Beauty: In the Eye of the Beholder?
New research shows that body mass index (BMI)—a ratio of weight scaled for height—is particularly important in mate selection. Moreover, the range of BMIs that males find attractive happens to be the same range that reflects optimal female health and fertility.

Scientific American Connection

Depression's Double Standard by Kristen Leutwyler (1997)
Studies from 10 nations reveal that the rates of depression among women are twice as high as they are among men. Do women have a biological bent for depression, or are social double standards the major cause? (See related activity)

Sex Differences in the Brain (1966)
There is increasing evidence that mammalian behavior patterns are basically female and that male patterns are induced by the action of the sex hormone testosterone on the brain of the newborn animal.

Sex Differences in the Brain (1992)
Cognitive variations between the sexes reflect differing hormonal influences on brain development. Understanding these differences and their causes can yield insights into brain organization.

Sex Differences in the Brain: Then and Now
In 1966, Seymour Levine published an article on sex differences in the brain. In 1992, after this area of research had become controversial and politicized, Doreen Kimura published an article with the identical title. In this activity, excerpts from these two articles are presented side by side, and students are asked to spot some differences in substance and style between these two articles separated by 26 years of intensive research. The activity also serves as a review of that to look for in reading a scientific article, and allows students to see the "self-correcting" nature of science in action. Note: This activity is intended to be done before you read the actual articles on which the activity is based.

Ask Dr. Mike

- What does Freud have to say about the development of homosexuality in men?
- Are there any differences between the male and female brain?
- I read an article recently where they said that having a "wet dream" was a normal experience and did not reflect a psychological disorder. Is this true or does it really reflect a disorder?
- Is there any evidence to suggest that homosexuality is due to "nature" rather than "nurture"?
- My friend and I have a bet and hope you can settle it for us. Who is better at lying, men or women?

Chapter Twelve
Personality

Learning Activities

Investigating Graphology: Is the Writing on the Wall?
Does your handwriting reveal true details of your personality? Explore the world of graphology, the art of handwriting analysis, in conjunction with the Scientific American Frontiers program, *Beyond Science*. Examine authentic writing samples, listen to a graphologist explain his craft, and do an experiment in graphology. Judge for yourself: Is graphology science or fact?

Investigating Dreams
Ever wonder about your crazy dreams? Would interpreting your dreams provide you with any special insights? Here's an opportunity to try it yourself and find out. First, review the prevalent dream theories, then, over a three-week period, record and interpret your own dreams. All the materials you'll need are provided here.

Op Ed Essays

Who or What is to Blame for the Littleton Massacre? by Kevin Byrd, University of Nebraska at Kearney
Is there one single cause for the tragedy at Columbine High School? What do we need to know about our teenagers? Clinical psychologist Kevin Byrd proposes some answers and invites you to post your views on the forum.

The Social Usefulness of Self-Esteem: A Skeptical View by Robyn M. Dawes, Carnegie Mellon University
In pop psychology, high self-esteem is often considered a major criterion of good mental health. But does psychological science support this premise? Robyn Dawes explores the research and offers a new view of the subject of self-esteem.

Ask Dr. Mike

- What are ink blots made out of and how are they made?
- In the Freudian structure of the mind, is it fair to say that the Id is "selfish," and that the Superego is "good?"
- Can a personality test ever be "wrong"?
- I've heard that aluminum may cause Alzheimer's Disease. Should I worry about drinking from aluminum cans?
- What's a "Freudian slip"?
- Where can I find various personality inventories on the Web?

Chapter Thirteen
Psychological Disorders

Learning Activities

Investigating Sex Differences in Depression
Is there a gender bias in depression? Become a part of an online study and discover the truth. Find out your score on the Self-Rating Depression Scale and compare your results with the study averages for your gender, then see how our results compare to the national averages.

Recognizing Mood Disorders
Would you like to explore mood disorders from the clinician's chair? After a brief review of depression and mania, this activity gives you the opportunity to "diagnose" six sample patients, based on brief case histories. Includes a link to the American Psychological Association's classification of mood disorders based on DSM-IV (*The Diagnostic and Statistical Manual*, 4th Edition).

Drug Use, Abuse, and Addictions: Focus on Alcohol
In this activity, you will examine where drug abuse and addictions begin with a special focus on alcohol and its use among young people today. You will engage in a debate on lowering the drinking age and keep track of your own substance use.

Research News

Editor's Note: Unabomber Update
The refusal by Kaczynski to allow an insanity defense puts that plea itself on trial: How disturbed must a personal be to qualify?

Schizophrenic Disorder: When People Hear Voices, Who's Talking?
For many people with schizophrenic disorder, auditory hallucinations—especially of other people's voices criticizing or commanding them—are among their most distressing experiences. Several lines of recent research are helping elucidate the brain functions and cognitive processes behind these voices, as well as providing practical techniques for decreasing the discomfort of hallucinatory experiences.

Eating Disorders and Sudden Death
It has been said that a woman can never be too thin or too rich. However, sometimes excessive thinness (or the manner of achieving it) can become a death sentence for women or men. Especially in the worlds of entertainment, modeling, and sports, women often feel pressured to be thin. A recent case shows how this drive for thinness can get out of control, emphasizing the dangerous consequences of eating disorders.

Mental Illness: Dangers, Treatment, and Civil Liberties
In July 1998, two police officers were killed at the United States Capitol by Russell Weston, Jr., who had been diagnosed earlier with paranoid schizophrenia. This act again raises the question of the connection between mental illness and violence: Is there truly a connection, and if there is, how should the mentally ill be treated? What are their civil rights? Do they conflict with the greater good of the community?

The Manic-Depressive Brain
Brain researchers using powerful imaging techniques have pinpointed an area of the brain involved in heritable forms of two relatively common mood disorders, depression and manic-depression. The brain area they observed, the subgenual prefontal cortex, has neural connections to other brain structures involved in emotional behavior and the body's physiological responses to emotion. Finding a link between the brain region and the mood disorders may help researchers to better understand and treat those conditions in the future.

DSM-IV: How Many Entries for The Book of Names?
The Diagnostic and Statistical Manual, 4th Edition (DSM-IV), published in 1994 by the American Psychiatric Association, is our nation's main classification system for mental disorders. The book is used by mental health professionals, governmental agencies, third-party health insurers, and researchers studying disordered behavior. DSM-IV includes more than 300 disorders—nearly triple the number listed just 18 years ago in the book's first edition. Are we growing more mentally dysfunctional? Or is the classification process itself proliferating? Supporters see the burgeoning of categories as a benefit to precision research. Some critics, however, view the DSM-IV as a "marketing machine" that financially benefits practitioners but siphons off funds needed for treating the most serious mental illnesses. Recent research articles highlight the debate over the Book of Names.

Teen Suicide—Symptom of a Changing World or Exaggerated Suggestibility in Adolescence?
Suicide is one of the most frequent causes of death, worldwide, in the adolescent age group. Psychologists have explained this phenomenon in various ways, including despair for the future and an enhanced suggestibility in adolescents. A recent case of six suicides, all by hanging, of young men from the same Boston community seems to illustrate several psychological phenomena.

The Insanity Defense and the Unabomber Trial

The trial of Unabomber suspect Theodore Kaczynski has brought the insanity defense back to public attention. Is Kaczynski a sane person who is accused of carrying out "crazy" actions or a mentally disturbed person who pretends to sanity? The insanity defense has a long but controversial history. Is it ever justified? Does "insanity" remove responsibility for a crime? How does this defense affect trial outcomes? Misconceptions about the insanity plea and its results are common, but recent scholarly articles help clear them up.

Beyond Shyness: Diagnosing and Treating Social Phobia

Social phobia, a devastating anxiety disorder that goes far beyond ordinary shyness, is the third most often diagnosed psychiatric disorder in the United States. Although antidepressant medication is now the prescribed treatment, psychological therapies may be as effective. Opponents to medication worry that people who are merely shy or socially uncomfortable may be treated with antidepressants, even though research has not demonstrated their effectiveness for these problems.

Does Being Female Increase Depression Risks for Females?

Can the way women think affect their tendency to become depressed? Researchers believe that women's ruminative thinking style may be the key to explaining why, from early adolescence on, they are more likely than men to report being depressed or to be diagnosed with depression.

Gambling as an Addictive Disorder

Most people in the United States consider some amount of gambling to be normal. But for some two and one half million adults and teenage Americans, gambling is a disabling disorder. About half the teenagers who experience serious gambling problems have pathological patterns of gambling activity or are serious compulsive gamblers. There is currently no clear, effective treatment for pathological gambling.

Prescription for Depression and PMS: Sleep Deprivation?

Both traditional wisdom and past psychological studies tell us that sleep deprivation is bad for your health and well-being. However, recent research suggests that sleep deprivation may be helpful in the treatment of depression and premenstrual syndrome. Despite preliminary evidence, sleep deprivation treatment remains controversial.

Understanding Schizophrenia: Where and When You Were Born Makes a Difference

Schizophrenia seems to result from a complex interaction of heredity and environment, but the exact causes are unclear. New research from Denmark adds some intriguing new risk factors to the puzzle.

Op Ed Essays

The Tragedy of Adolescent Suicide—Finding Options for Prevention

Suicide is a major cause of death among children and adolescents. Unfortunately, suicide rates for adolescents and young adults are increasing dramatically. What societal factors serve to exacerbate adolescent suicide rates? What individual risk factors are involved? In this Op-Ed feature Barbara Sarason provides illuminating answers to these questions and addresses the challenges of suicide prevention. Her expertise and sensitivity provide an overview and excellent insight into this relevant and disturbing topic.

Scientific American Connection

Manic-Depressive Illness and Creativity by Kay Redfield Jamison (1995)

Does some fine madness plague great artists? Several studies now show that creativity and mood disorders are linked. (See related activity)

Depression's Double Standard by Kristen Leutwyler (1997)
Studies from 10 nations reveal that the rates of depression among women are twice as high as they are among men. Do women have a biological bent for depression, or are social double standards the major cause? (See related activity)

Ask Dr. Mike

- What is antisocial personality disorder? Can this explain the Littleton shootings?
- What is an "anxiety attack?"
- What is bipolar disease, and how do you get it? What are some symptoms, and is there a cure?
- Can psychological blindness correct itself?
- What is Tourette's Syndrome?
- What is "normal," anyway? If reality is based on perception, how can we label a schizophrenic as "abnormal?"
- Is it typical to feel "down" after reading or talking about depression?
- What is the likelihood that the genes for a mental disorder can be passed down from your parents? Would the home environment have any effect?
- With multiple personality disorder, can one of the personalities be ill while the other is healthy?
- Concerning Tourette's Syndrome, does a person have inappropriate behaviors other than swearing, such as inappropriate sexual behavior in public?
- Is Anorexia Nervosa really a form of anxiety disorder?
- What is Luvox?
- Are there any patterns, symptoms, or characteristics of children and wives who are abused?
- Can children develop schizophrenia?
- Can you become addicted to the Internet?
- I have a history of bipolar disorder in my family. How can I tell the difference between everyday mood swings and real disorder?
- I've heard that depression is not a thought disorder. However, if a depressed person considers suicide, isn't that an example of a thought disorder?
- I've heard that Prozac has few, if any, side effects. Is this true?
- If a child is born with a mental disorder are there fewer folds in the child's brain?
- In dissociative identity disorder, can one personality be "blind" while the others have normal vision?
- Is alcoholism genetic?
- Is it common for autistic children to have one "outstanding" ability?
- Is it considered abnormal to sometimes have feelings of depression and consider suicide?
- Is lithium the only drug treatment for bipolar disorder?
- Is there a relationship between a full moon and mental disorders?
- Is there such a thing as borderline personality disorder?
- My boyfriend has schizotypal personality disorder. He is seeing a psychiatrist and is taking an antipsychotic. Do you know of any available treatments other than medication?
- What are conversion disorders? What causes them and how do you treat them?
- What are some of the causes of depression? How can you climb out of depression?
- What causes dyslexia?
- What is dysgraphia?

- What is it called if you are afraid of sex?
- What is narcolepsy? And can narcolepsy affect your sex life?
- What is serotonin?
- What is the difference between psychosis and neurosis?
- What was wrong with Jack Nicholson in the movie, "As Good as It Gets"?
- What's the difference between a neurosis and a psychosis?

Chapter Fourteen
Therapy

Research News

Feeling Low This Winter? "A Sunny Disposition" May Help
Many people experience "winter doldrums" brought on by fewer hours of daylight in the winter months. For some, however, the symptoms are more extreme and constitute a true Seasonal Affective Disorder or SAD. Young adult women are typical sufferers, but children and adolescents can show signs of SAD, as well. An effective treatment is exposure to special, very bright, lighting. Researchers are learning more about treating this disorder, as well as why it may occur.

Childhood and Adolescent Depression—To Medicate or Not?
Before 1980, few clinicians believed in childhood depression. Today, mental health professionals not only recognize depressive disorders in children but agree that these conditions can persist and can have severe consequences. Despite the proven benefits of psychotherapy for treating childhood depression, physicians prescribed Prozac and related antidepressants to nearly 600,000 children in 1996. This represents a substantial increase over 1995 prescription levels, and it came despite a paucity of solid data on the utility and long-term effects of these relatively new drugs for young people. How should professionals make treatment decisions for depressed kids and teens?

Beyond Shyness: Diagnosing and Treating Social Phobia
Social phobia, a devastating anxiety disorder that goes far beyond ordinary shyness, is the third most often diagnosed psychiatric disorder in the United States. Although antidepressant medication is now the prescribed treatment, psychological therapies may be as effective. Opponents to medication worry that people who are merely shy or socially uncomfortable may be treated with antidepressants, even though research has not demonstrated their effectiveness for these problems.

Prescription for Depression and PMS: Sleep Deprivation?
Both traditional wisdom and past psychological studies tell us that sleep deprivation is bad for your health and well-being. However, recent research suggests that sleep deprivation may be helpful in the treatment of depression and premenstrual syndrome. Despite preliminary evidence, sleep deprivation treatment remains controversial.

Psychoactive Drugs for Children: Panacea or Peril?
Over three million children in the United States are currently taking Ritalin, more than double the number in 1990. An additional estimated 580,000 children are currently being prescribed antidepressants. With more than 4 four million children taking powerful drugs to manage their behavior, a major controversy is brewing among professionals concerned with the health and welfare of children.

Scientific American Connection

Depression's Double Standard by Kristen Leutwyler (1997)
Studies from 10 nations reveal that the rates of depression among women are twice as high as they are among men. Do women have a biological bent for depression, or are social double standards the major cause? (See related activity)

Ask Dr. Mike

- In a counterconditioning procedure, can you get a transfer of fear to the positive stimulus rather than the other way around?
- What is Luvox?
- Is electroconvulsive therapy (ECT) always beneficial?
- I've heard that Prozac has few, if any, side effects. Is this true?
- Is it common to mix treatments for various disorders, for example, electroconvulsive therapy (ECT) and lithium?
- Can biofeedback help combat depression?
- Can psychological blindness correct itself?
- Does serotonin have an effect on depression? Can it induce self-harm?
- I have been on Prozac for about 6 to 8 months now, and I have been having very violent and disturbing dreams. Could this be a side effect of the Prozac?
- If the neurotransmitter serotonin enhances mood, how is it related to depression?
- Is it true that the person who "invented" the lobotomy was killed by one of his patients?
- Is lithium the only drug treatment for bipolar disorder?
- My boyfriend has schizotypal personality disorder. He is seeing a psychiatrist and is taking an antipsychotic. Do you know of any available treatments other than medication?
- What benefit has amantadine shown in people post TBI?
- What can you tell me about Ritalin?
- What is Gestalt Therapy?

Chapter Fifteen
Health Psychology

Research News

Classes, Computers, Exams . . . and Beer: College Drinking
Is drinking on college campuses a serious problem? For several decades the incidence of student drinking on college campuses has been studied with mixed findings. More recent studies indicate a higher incidence of binge drinking than expected in large mixed-sex college settings. These findings indicate that these drinking patterns are related to a higher incidence of academic, social, and legal problems. Students who binge-drink are also at risk for physical problems due to poor health-related behaviors such as cigarette smoking, abuse of other substances, and unplanned sex.

Coping After Abortion

New research by Brenda Major and her colleagues explores how personal resilience, cognitive appraisals, and coping efforts work together to determine postabortion adjustment. In their longitudinal study of 527 women who underwent first-trimester abortions, they found most of the women to be well-adjusted and satisfied with their decision. Women with resilient personalities appraised their experience more positively, viewing their abortion as less stressful and having confidence in their ability to cope with the abortion. Their more positive view of the experience led to more successful coping strategies. The researchers concluded that teaching more beneficial forms of coping would be a useful clinical intervention for women adjusting poorly after an abortion.

Procrastination May be Dangerous to Your Health and Performance

When facing a deadline far in the future, procrastination may succeed as a way to reduce stress. In the long run, however, procrastinators may be making themselves sick! Recent research with college students shows that those who self-identified as procrastinators early in the semester felt more stressed as a deadline approached. They also experienced more physical symptoms and visited health care professionals more often. Procrastination seems to hurt performance, too: Delaying assigned work correlated positively with lower grades on both an assigned paper and on exams.

Getting Old: Better Than You Expect

Most of us joke and worry about growing older, but many of our fears are unjustified. The authors of three articles in a recent issue of *Science* present data on the influence of genes, the longevity of neurons, and the fluctuations of hormones on our health as we age. Their findings are positive and their message encouraging.

Maternal Grooming: A Lifelong Aid to Stress Reduction?

Researchers at McGill University in Montreal have discovered that rats literally groom their young for success—success in resisting the negative effects of stress. High levels of maternal licking and grooming lead to adult offspring with a healthier physiological response to stress, freer tendencies to explore, and a greater ability to overcome anxiety. Are there human lessons to be learned from their maternal instincts?

Rethinking the Power of Positive Thinking

Both the popular press and research psychologists have paid substantial attention to the power of positive thinking (optimism). However, four researchers at Ohio State University have now reported that avoiding negative thinking (pessimism) may be even more important than striving for optimism when it comes to physical and psychological health. In a longitudinal study of adults, the team examined the relationships between negative life events, optimism, pessimism, and subjects' perception of their own stress, depression, anxiety, and physical health. About half of the participants were under extreme stress from caring for a relative with Alzheimer's disease. The Ohio team found that in nonstressed adults, optimism and pessimism were largely independent of each other; this was less true among the individuals coping with high stress levels. Further, it was pessimism, not optimism, that uniquely predicted psychological and physical health for both stressed and nonstressed groups. Future research is needed to determine whether the benefits of optimism accrue directly from positive thinking or from avoiding negative thinking—or perhaps some combination of the two.

Cigarette Smoking and Genetics: A Not So Unlikely Combination (3/29/98)

Why is it easy for some people to quit smoking, while others can't seem to kick the habit? Why do some people start smoking in the first place? New research suggests that part of the answer to these questions may lie in the presence or absence of specific genes. More information about genes identified with smoking risk can ultimately identify who is at risk for nicotine dependence and can help determine the best way to quit smoking.

Does Cigarette Smoking Increase Stress Rather Than Reduce It

Even though smoking cigarettes is known to be hazardous, there is a widely held belief that is has positive emotional effects. Smoking is presumed to help a person relax. However, recent research suggest that the opposite may be true—smoking increases stress rather than reduces it.

Is NYC Dangerous to Your Health?

Stress can be harmful to your health, and New York City is a stressful place to live. The rate of heart disease in New York City is higher than the national average, but that higher rate could have many causes. Does something about exposure to New York City, for residents and visitors, lead to a high death rate from ischemic heart disease?

Leptin: Weight Loss Panacea or Pipe Dream?

Obesity is a health-threatening crisis of epidemic proportions in the U.S. and other countries around the world in which people consume large amounts of fast foods. The hormone leptin may provide a promising treatment for obesity by signaling the body to reduce fat accumulation. Although the media reported that a recent large-scale clinical trial of leptin confirmed its promise, a closer reading of the study reveals problems.

Perils of Hostile Feelings: Heart Disease and an Expanding Waistline

Hostile feelings may have a negative impact not only on social relationships, but on appearance and length of life as well. People who feel hostile or angry toward others may be setting up a vulnerability for stroke or heart attack in their future. In addition, at least for men, the changes in adrenal gland secretion that accompany hostility tend to create overweight, especially excess fat around the waistline and abdomen, by middle age.

Regrets? . . . I've Had a Few: Women's Midlife Review and Well-Being

Until recently, social scientists have tended to view midlife as a developmental stage that requires a major adaptation—especially for women, who must deal with the negative stereotypes associated with aging women. Contemporary studies have begun to focus on the midlife adaptations of women by examining their regrets about choices in early life, and whether making relevant changes in midlife is related to differences in adjustment.

Sharing Secrets: Siblings and Self-Disclosure

A recent study investigated the ways in which adult brothers and sisters share highly personal and confidential information. It found some essential differences between how we share our secrets with friends and with siblings, and underscored the importance of a good sibling relationship to lifelong support.

Social Control: Good and Bad for Your Health

Changing a bad habit is never easy. Friends and family may urge you to adopt healthy behaviors, such as exercising regularly, or giving up smoking; but does their urging, no matter how well-intentioned, really help? A new study of "social control" has uncovered some answers that should make loved ones reconsider their efforts.

Teens at Risk Across Cultures: Sex, Drugs, and AIDS

Recent research indicates that teens who had knowledge about AIDS and how to reduce the risk of AIDS were just as likely to combine sexual behaviors with substance abuse as those who did not have such awareness. These high-risk behaviors occurred with different frequencies among different ethnic groups. Understanding why high-risk behaviors occur at different rates among different ethnic groups may provide critical information needed to develop effective strategies for reducing the risk of AIDS among adolescents.

The Shape of Beauty: In the Eye of the Beholder?

New research shows that body mass index (BMI)—a ratio of weight scaled for height—is particularly important in mate selection. Moreover, the range of BMIs that males find attractive happens to be the same range that reflects optimal female health and fertility.

Why Dieters Fail—They Don't Mind Eating When Their Minds Are Elsewhere
At any one time 40% of women and 25% of men report that they are on a diet to control their weight. Only about one in 20 people who make an initial attempt at dieting, however, succeed. Why is it that most dieters don't succeed even if they try, try, and try again? According to one cognitive theory, they simply may not be paying attention to their eating in certain kinds of involving situations.

Women with Cancer: When the Caregiver Requires Care
The American Cancer Society currently estimates that one in three women in America will develop cancer over the course of their lives. Although cancer is a disease that affects both men and women, when mothers of young children develop cancer the consequences are far-reaching. Recent research shows that a high degree of mutuality in the relationship between a woman cancer patient and her partner helps the patient engage in self-care, improves her quality of life, protects her from depression, and facilitates the overall adjustment of the family.

Ask Dr. Mike

- Does stress help us to remember information (like phone numbers) or does it make us forget?
- Can meditation heal?
- Are cigarette smokers physically and psychologically addicted to smoking? How are they physically addicted? How are they psychologically addicted?
- Can mental attitude influence a biological disease?
- Can repeated exposure to stress result in an autoimmune disease?
- I've heard stories that a sexually transmitted disease such as syphilis can make you crazy. Is this true? If so, how does it happen?
- Is it possible to switch between being a Type A and a Type B personality?
- It seems to me that people spend a long time looking up at the floor indicators in an elevator. What's going on?
- What is a migraine headache?

Chapter Sixteen
Social Psychology: The Individual in Society

Learning Activities

Investigating Social Judgments: Expectations, Stereotypes, and the Impressions We're Left With
In this interactive activity, you discover how stereotypes influence our impressions of others. You will participate in actual research related to social and cognitive psychology. An assessment exercise is included to see your own results.

Investigating Gangs and Behavior
What are gangs? What motivates adolescents to join them? And how can we discourage gang membership? Learn the answers to these questions and discover why social and developmental psychologists are interested in this phenomenon. Through various activities, you will explore statistics, propose prevention to parents, and design an ideal program to discourage gang involvement.

Exploring Academic Dishonesty

Academic dishonesty, or cheating, is not uncommon in today's colleges and universities. But when does cheating begin? What motivates students to cheat? And can anything be done to stop it? Learn more about the issues and research regarding this highly publicized topic and do your own research using the activities provided.

Research News

Predicting Our Own Social Behavior

New research by Janet Swim and Lauri Hyers reminds us again why we need social psychological research—to discover not just how people think they will act, but how (and why) they do act as they do.

Another Explanation for Differences in Intellectual Performance: Stereotype Threat

Claude Steele (1997) suggests that negative stereotypes about women and African Americans may impair their performance in the classroom and on standardized tests. Steele also suggests that stereotype threat may be responsible for underperformance in the classroom by students from these same two groups. Additionally, he suggests that stereotyped groups may use disidentification, which serves to protect their self-esteem.

Racism Requires Racial Categorization

Social identity theory predicts that people who strongly identify with an in-group will maintain clear boundaries with relevant out-groups. Psychologist Jim Blascovich and his colleagues predicted, and found, that prejudiced people take more time to carefully categorize people whose race is ambiguous.

Juvenile Violence: Why the Mass Murder at Jonesboro, Arkansas?

Following the recent mass murder in Jonesboro, Arkansas, involving alleged assailants just 11 and 13 years old, the media and general public posed many questions concerning juvenile violence. A recent article in *American Psychologist* explores these complex questions and summarizes five major misconceptions and controversies surrounding violence in youngsters.

When "Harmless" Flirtation Hurts

When does a college flirtation cease being harmless fun and start causing damage? It's when your professor is doing the flirting, say psychologists Arthur Satterfield and Charlene Muehlenhard. In two new studies, they examine the effects of an authority figure's flirtatious behavior on college women and how these students then see their own creative performance. The work explores a "gray area" of sexual harassment, and demonstrates how minor flirtation can shake a woman's self-confidence and sense of achievement.

The Social Consequences of Affirmative Action

Affirmative action programs have created important opportunities for individuals who experience societal discrimination and disadvantage. Such programs are controversial, however, and some have suggested that those who benefit from affirmative action also pay a price in terms of unfavorable attitudes about their capabilities. A new study by two social psychologists from Canada and Wales supports this: They examined public attitudes about a new, relatively unfamiliar, immigrant group, Surinamers, before and after exposure to a media campaign. The information they disseminated was always positive but sometimes included a mention of the group's eligibility for affirmative action. Their results show that the existence of affirmative action affects attitudes towards both the groups and specific individuals who would benefit from such programs.

Can Subliminal Messages Manipulate the Subconscious and Behavior?

A recent political advertisement flashed the word "RATS" briefly on television screens in the context of criticizing the opponent's position. Although it may have been intended as a joke, presenting a message so briefly that it is not perceived consciously is precisely the point of subliminal mind control—if it works.

Even Good People Can Be Moral Hypocrites

Unethical and immoral behavior is very much in the news today. Many people who engage in unethical acts are still able to feel that they behaved ethically. Research suggests that good people will fail to act morally or ethically because they unconsciously use self-deception strategies that enable them to maintain a positive self-concept.

How Stereotypes Affect Test Performance

Women are generally considered to be "not so good in math," while men are generally supposed to be "good in math." But is it true? Recent research shows that both negative and positive stereotypes about math ability may affect the performance of men and women on math tests.

Random Acts of Hate: Mental Disorder, Economic Conditions, or Organizational Membership?

Violent crimes against people because of their race, religious affiliation, sexual orientation, or some other characteristic seem to be increasing. A well-known psychiatrist has argued that this kind of extreme racism is a sign of mental illness. Others offer economic disparities or preoccupation with social change as explanations for hate crimes. Not everyone who has feelings of hate harms other people or their property. What makes the difference?

Social Control: Good and Bad for Your Health

Changing a bad habit is never easy. Friends and family may urge you to adopt healthy behaviors, such as exercising regularly, or giving up smoking; but does their urging, no matter how well-intentioned, really help? A new study of "social control" has uncovered some answers that should make loved ones reconsider their efforts.

Violent Video Game Play Increases Aggression

The popularity of violent video games has grown to phenomenal proportions. Users may experience more exposure to violence from playing video games than they experience from movies. Video game exposure can be longer and more frequent, and it involves not just passively watching, but also getting into the act. Two new studies scientifically assess the potential of these amusements to encourage violent and destructive behaviors in their users.

We Are All Better Than Average

Incompetent individuals often overestimate their abilities, while competent people tend to underestimate their abilities. Research suggests that we are not only poor judges of our abilities, but also overly optimistic about potential risks. Do incompetent people really have no clue that they are incompetent?

Op Ed Essays

A Psychologist Looks at the Death Penalty by Mark Costanzo, Claremont McKenna College

Did Karla Faye Tucker's recent execution in Texas serve any constructive purpose? Surveys show that many Americans, virtually alone among people across the industrialized world, believe capital punishment does serve a purpose. Are they right? Mark Costanzo, Chair of the Claremont McKenna College psychology department, has written many articles about capital punishment and has just published a provocative and well-argued book, *Just Revenge: Costs and Consequences of the Death Penalty* (St. Martin's Press). Here he gives us a sneak preview of what research shows. Does his evidence and reasoning persuade you that capital punishment just doesn't work? (Mark's book also engages other issues, such as: Does capital punishment save money? Is it moral? Do Americans support the death penalty?)

Are We Sugarcoating Culture? Thinking Critically About the Study of Diversity by Carole Wade, Dominican College of San Rafael

"Of course I dislike the Nazis," students have recently been heard to say, "but who is to say they were morally wrong? That was a different time and culture." Similarly, in our age of postmodernism and extreme relativism, some students allow respect for cultural diversity to invalidate judgments regarding ethnic cleansing, genital mutilation, and even slavery and human sacrifice. Their expressed nonjudgmentalism provokes Carole Wade, in this crisp and lucid essay, to wonder: Must multiculturalism neutralize moral judgment?

Organized Religion as a Human Universal
Is organized religion a human universal? Why might almost all civilizations have developed organized religions? Explore the issues with Sabah Hassan, winner of *The Psychology Place* Student Op Ed Contest!

The Mathematics of Beauty
When you are attracted to someone, is a mathematical ratio at the root of your attraction? Find out in The Mathematics of Beauty, by Kristin Saunders, our first STUDENT Op Ed author!

What Makes a Good Leader?
Is there a single trait that all good leaders possess? Robert J. Sternberg of Yale University offers a new approach to leadership and invites you to post your views on this topic in the forum.

Ask Dr. Mike

- Did TV violence cause the Littleton situation?
- Is the unresponsive-bystander effect only found in North America?
- What do people usually say when they are asked why they failed to help at an emergency situation?
- Is Frosh Week based at least partly on deindividuation?
- Does conformity play any role in jury decisions?
- Why is timing of the requests so important when using the door-in-the-face technique?
- During times of international conflict, does prejudice within a single country decrease?
- Were people obedient in the Milgram study because they somehow believed that the experimenter was "good," and would not let them do something harmful?
- What about the effects of watching real violence on TV, for example, on the evening news? Are the results the same as with fictional acts of aggression?
- Is altruism related to religion, e.g., would a more religious person be less susceptible to bystander effects?
- I've often heard that "opposites attract." Is this true? Are people who are opposite in physical attractiveness likely to get along?
- It seems likely that media violence can influence aggression, but why are people "drawn" to media violence? Is this some kind of natural drive?
- Are there any differences between individual and group decision making?
- Attractiveness is an important factor in changing attitudes. So how do you explain "social marketing"—ads that try to get you to contribute to various causes. The people in these ads are not necessarily attractive.
- Do we find a potential mate attractive because we are thinking (unconsciously) about how attractive our children might be?
- Does the way a teacher dresses have any effect on how much you respect them?
- Does violence on TV make children do violent things? Do children get ideas from TV or do they think what they see on TV is real?

- I don't understand Cognitive Dissonance Theory. Can you help?
- If you change an attitude, how long will the change last?
- In the Milgram experiment, why didn't the participants just leave? Aren't you free to leave a study at any time?
- The success of "reality TV" suggests that we enjoy watching real people in extraordinary situations. Why then do we still prefer beautiful people in advertising?
- What is the "small world" effect?
- What is the significance of eye contact in human interaction?
- When considering the effects of watching violence in the media, does the type of violence you watch matter? For example, I was depressed after watching "Saving Private Ryan," but relatively excited after watching "The Matrix."
- Who was Stanley Milgram?
- Why do you sometimes feel that the eyes of a person in a painting are "following" you?
- Would a person, opposed to gambling because of his religion, feel a lot of dissonance if he gambles anyway and loses a lot of money?

Chapter Seventeen
Industrial and Organizational Psychology

Research News

Ingratiation May Be Considered Slimy But It May Have Its Rewards

People who are nice to superiors but difficult with subordinates are often perceived as "slimy" by others, according to recent research. In addition, research suggests that although people who ingratiate themselves with their bosses are disliked by others, these slimy people have a slight edge in being advanced professionally than those who don't.

The Social Consequences of Affirmative Action

Affirmative action programs have created important opportunities for individuals who experience societal discrimination and disadvantage. Such programs are controversial, however, and some have suggested that those who benefit from affirmative action also pay a price in terms of unfavorable attitudes about their capabilities. A new study by two social psychologists from Canada and Wales supports this: They examined public attitudes about a new, relatively unfamiliar, immigrant group, Surinamers, before and after exposure to a media campaign. The information they disseminated was always positive but sometimes included a mention of the group's eligibility for affirmative action. Their results show that the existence of affirmative action affects attitudes towards both the groups and specific individuals who would benefit from such programs.

Mentoring in the Workplace: Is it Worth the Effort?

Organizations are investing time and money in career development of new employees through mentoring programs. These programs are designed to help new employees advance in their careers and to facilitate better social adjustment within the organization. Research suggests that mentoring, especially informal mentoring, can lead to improved career development, greater job satisfaction, and more income for the person being mentored.

Op Ed Forum

What Makes a Good Leader?
Is there a single trait that all good leaders possess? Robert J. Sternberg of Yale University offers a new approach to leadership and invites you to post your views on this topic in the forum.

Ask Dr. Mike

- Does conformity play any role in jury decisions?

Thinking Critically About Video Classics in Psychology

CD-ROM to accompany Davis and Palladino, *Psychology, Third Edition: Media & Research Update*

John H. Krantz
Hanover College

CD-ROM Table of Contents

Chapter 1: Psychology, Research, and You

Video Title: *Controlling an Experiment—Konrad Lorenz*
Text Section: Research Methods in Psychology: The Experimental Method
Text Page: 19

Introduction

Various types of research methods are used to describe, predict, and explain behavior. The experiment is the only research method that is able to explain a relationship between variables. This is done by establishing causal connections between variables. In an experiment, the researcher actively controls the variables in a situation and measures the subject's behavior. In this video clip, Konrad Lorenz discusses the basic model of the experiment.

Make a Hypothesis:

- What do you think is the purpose of an experiment?

- In an experiment, any differences in behavior can be logically traced back to what feature of the experiment?

  Answer: The independent variable is the variable that the researcher manipulates in an experiment. It is "independent" of any other factors. The purpose of an experiment is to test a hypothesis by manipulating the independent variable, keeping other aspects of the experimental situation constant, and observing behavior. Thus, any differences can be traced back to the experiment.

The Video in Perspective

- What is the basic model of an experiment?

  Suggested Answer: All experiments seek to control conditions and have only the independent variable change. That way the changes in the dependent variable can be attributed to the independent variable.

- What are two essential elements of true experiments?

  Suggested Answer: You need to control the environment and manipulate the independent variable.

Psychological Detective

- Konrad Lorenz is talking about "unobtrusive experiments." How are these different from the experiments discussed in the text? What are some of the advantages of "unobtrusive experiments" vs. laboratory experiments?

  Suggested Answer: Lorenz is talking about trying to change as little as possible of the natural environment. They are different in that they try to make the situation as natural as possible or actually do them in the field where laboratory experiments are done in artificial settings to gain control. Some advantages come in terms of the validity of the finding. By keeping as much of the natural setting as possible you know that your independent variable works in the natural environment.

Chapter 2: Biological Foundations of Psychology

Video Title: *Electrical Brain Stimulation*
Text Section: **The Nervous System: The Central Nervous System: The Brain**
Text Page: 52

Introduction

One research method used in brain research is to invade the brain through *experimental intervention* and then measure the effects on behavior. One invasive technique is to "lesion" a part of the brain by surgically destroying it. Another technique is to administer drugs that are suspected of having effects on neurotransmitters and other activity in the brain. A third type of intervention is through the use of *electrical brain stimulation*. Here, a microelectrode is inserted in the brain and a mild electrical current activates the neurons in a particular site. Brain surgeons "map" the patient's brain so that key functions are not destroyed. The patient is given a local anesthetic and kept awake for the procedure.

While neurosurgeon Wilder Penfield operated on hundreds of epileptic patients back in the 1940s, he stimulated exposed parts of the cortex with a tiny electric probe, "mapping" the human cortex. Penfield discovered that certain areas of the brain specialize in receiving sensory information. Penfield stimulated different areas along the surface of the brain and found that, depending on the region he stimulated, the patients would report visual images, tingling sensations, muscular twitches, and other reactions. Much of what is currently known about the functions of the four lobes in the cerebral cortex come from Penfield's early work in "mapping" various locations in the cortex that house sensory and motor functions.

Make a Hypothesis

- What will happen when Penfield stimulates a small area of the temporal lobe, called the auditory cortex?

  Answer: Different regions of the brain are involved with different functions of our mind and body. This is one way that the brain can accomplish all of the tasks it has to do. The auditory cortex is the first part of the brain that is involved in hearing, so when it is stimulated, the person should hear something.

The Video in Perspective

- What four types of research methods are commonly used in the study of behavioral neuroscience?

  Suggested Answer: Anatomy, recording, stimulation, lesion.

Psychological Detective

- Why should it matter where the electrical brain stimulation occurs? What are the functions of the somatosensory cortex, motor cortex, and association cortex areas? How do these functions relate to what Penfield finds in his electrical brain stimulation studies?

  Suggested Answer: It matters where the stimulation occurs because different parts of the brain are involved in different functions. The somatosensory cortex receives sensory information from the skin and body, the motor cortex is an important movement center and association cortexes are older terms for regions of the brain that process more complicated features of our mental activities. These regions give predictable response to the stimulation by Penfield.

Chapter 3: Sensation and Perception

Video Title: *Visual Cliff*
Text Section: Perception: Basic Perceptual Abilities: Patterns and Constancies
Text Page: 125

Introduction

Eleanor Gibson and Richard Walk conducted an experiment in 1960 to determine whether the ability to perceive depth is inborn or learned. They devised the "visual cliff" to study depth perception. The visual cliff is an apparatus that consists of a glass-covered table top with a shallow drop on one end and a steep "cliff" on the other end. At the edge of the shallow side is the appearance of a sudden drop-off; however, the entire surface is covered by glass.

Make a Hypothesis

- Do you think the babies will crawl to their mothers over the deep end? In other words, will they crawl out over the cliff?

  Answer: The babies can see through to the floor below. They may feel the plexiglass, but once they have some experience moving around, they will have had the experience of falling and know that falling hurts. Once the babies can crawl, it might well be that their experience of falling will overcome their feel of the clear plexiglass, of which they do not have experience, and they will not crawl to their mothers.

The Video in Perspective

- Do you think that the results of the study prove that the ability to perceive depth is innate rather than learned? Why or why not?

  Suggested Answer: No, because these babies all can crawl and that does not occur until about the 6th to 7th month. The ability still might not have been present at birth.

Psychological Detective

- These babies refuse to cross to their mothers over the glass side. Why? What basic perceptual ability(ies) must be involved in these babies refusal to cross the glass?

  Suggested Answer: The babies must be able to perceive depth to know that the floor is a long way down.

Video Title: *Perceptual Hypothesis: Pointing*
Text Section: Perceptual Hypotheses and Illusions
Text Page: 128

Introduction

Hermann von Helmholtz, one of the greatest scientists of the nineteenth century, is remembered in psychology for his contributions both to the study of sensation and his studies of the nervous system. In his work on perception, Helmholtz emphasized the role of experience in perception. He argued that we use prior experience about the environment to make inferences or hypotheses about the way things really are. He called these hypotheses unconscious inferences. Such inferences about objects seem to be made automatically. We are normally unaware of making such perceptual inference because we are so highly practiced at and so often accurate in making these inferences.

In this experiment, Charles Harris studies how the use of distortion goggles affect the subject's vision. The subject is first shown a rod in front of her and asked to point to it. She correctly does so. Next, the subject puts on the distortion goggles that display what she sees over to the right. Charles Harris shows the subject that she points about 14 degrees to the right. Then he asks the subject to keep pointing to where the rod is now located.

Make a Hypothesis:

- As the subject keeps repeating the pointing what will happen to her ability to point correctly? What will happen after the goggles are removed to the subject's ability to point?

  Answer: One of the most important ways we get around is our vision. It is a vital feature of how we are able to move and grasp objects. If we shift the appearance of an object, we should point to where it appears and not where it is. But when the person can see this error, they can correct their reaching, eventually grasping the object correctly. However, when the goggles come off, the subject should not point too far in the opposite direction.

The Video in Perspective

- What does this video imply about the role of learning in our perceptions?

  Suggested Answer: The ability to coordinate movement with perception has a heavily learned component. By using visual feedback the subject was able to point accurately with the distorting prism in the way.

Psychological Detective

- Compare this result to the visual cliff video. Do both videos have the same thing to say about the role of innate versus learned elements in our perceptions?

  Suggested Answer: This video indicates that there is a heavily learned component about the way we integrate movement with perception. Combining this with the visual cliff, it says that part of the reason the babies did not cross is that they knew that falling would hurt. This may take experience to be able to make this connection.

Chapter 4: Motivation and Emotions

Video Title: **Reinforcement versus Achievement**
Text Section: **Specific Motives: Achievement**
Text Page: **157**

Introduction

Psychologists who specialize in industrial and organizational psychology have studied work motivation. David McClelland has studied people with a need for achievement, defined as a learned motive to meet personal standards of success and excellence in a chosen area. There is a strong association among a person's motivation, behavior, and level of accomplishment. Those who score high in the need for achievement work harder, are more persistent, innovative, and future-oriented than those who score low in the need for achievement. In addition, high scorers desire success more than they fear failure and then credit their success to internal factors (such as ability and effort) rather than to external factors. In this video clip, B.F. Skinner explains achievement motivation in behavioral terms.

Make a Hypothesis

- How would you expect a behaviorist to explain achievement motivation?

  Answer: B. F. Skinner explains most of behavior as resulting from our history of reinforcements. So achievement motivation should be a result of having been reinforced for achieving in the past.

The Video in Perspective

- If Skinner is correct that achievement motivation is due to reinforcement, then should a person's achievement level stay fairly constant over life, or would it be able to be changed?

  Suggested Answer: It would depend upon the person's reinforcement history. If the person is consistently reinforced for achievement, the motivation would stay high. If the reinforcement fluctuates, then so would the achievement motivation.

Psychological Detective

- How might you test whether McClelland or Skinner are correct in their beliefs about achievement motivation? What do these two different views say about the way we work?

  Suggested Answer: You would need to change the reinforcers—for example, reward people for not achieving. Would that lower achievement motivation? Achievement motivation would suggest that those with high achievement motivation work to fulfill this internal drive. Skinner would say we work because of the reinforcement history of getting paid and the social reinforcers that go along with working.

Video Title:	***Motivation as seen by Carl Rogers***
Text Section:	**Specific Motives: Achievement**
Text Page:	**157**

Introduction

Motivation is an internal state that accounts for the arousal, direction, and persistence of behavior. The study of motivation is of interest not only to the field of psychology. A number of questions, such as studying what motivates people to excel, what motivates people to commit violent crimes, and everyday motivational states, such as regulating hunger and sexual arousal, are relevant to many other fields of study.

In this video clip, Dr. Carl Rogers discusses his theory of motivation. Carl Rogers is a part of the so-called third force in psychology, known as humanistic psychology. This approach is based on the premise that there is value in the individual's search for growth. Another humanist psychologist, Abraham Maslow, proposed that human motives could be ranked from basic survival needs to needs for self-actualization. Maslow contended that needs must be met at each level before moving on to higher-level needs.

Make a Hypothesis

- What do you think will be the central factor in motivation according to Carl Rogers?

  Answer: Carl Rogers believes that we self-actualize by trying to bring our true self and perceived selves into line with our ideal self. So motivation is an inherent biological need to be what we should be.

The Video in Perspective

- What does Carl Rogers think about the concept of achievement motivation? Is he like B. F. Skinner in this regard?

  Suggested Answer: He sees this concept as simply one feature of our drive towards growth and not a specific drive. Both Rogers and Skinner think that the idea of a specific achievement motivation does not make sense and that it is really part of a more fundamental process. The two processes are different, however. For Rogers it is growth and for Skinner it is reinforcement.

- How is Rogers' perspective on motivation similar to Maslow's? How is it different from other theories of motivation (biological, cognitive, humanistic, learning)?

  Suggested Answer: Both are humanistic psychologists and as such share many common concerns, such as for growth. But fore Maslow, self-actualization is the greatest motivation, while for Rogers it is to be authentic. Both however differ in that they see motivation driving the person towards growth and not merely fulfilling needs or the result of reinforcement history as some other theories do.

Video Title: *Human Emotion*
Text Section: **The What and the Why of Emotion**
Text Page: **160**

Introduction

Emotion is defined as a state of arousal involving facial and bodily changes, brain activation, cognitive appraisals, subjective feelings, and tendencies toward action. Following Darwin's work, Psychologist Paul Ekman and his colleagues have identified seven basic facial expressions of emotion that are recognized the world over: anger, happiness, fear, surprise, disgust, sadness, and contempt. In this video clip, B.F. Skinner discusses the usefulness of the concept of emotion.

Make a Hypothesis

- Do you think B.F. Skinner would say emotion is a useful concept? Why or why not?

  Answer: B. F. Skinner is a behaviorist. Behaviorists do not like to make explanations of behavior using internal constructions such as emotions. Thus, Skinner would not seek emotion as a useful concept in explaining behavior.

The Video in Perspective

- Do Skinner's ideas about emotion agree with the studies you read in the book on emotion?

  Suggested Answer: The student should discuss the expression of emotion, which Skinner ignores. Also our ability to measure internal states has grown tremendously since Skinner's time.

Psychological Detective

- How does Skinner define emotion? Why does he think that knowledge of internal states will not help us understand emotions?

  Suggested Answer: Emotions are a change in the probability of engaging in certain behaviors. For example, anger is the heightened probability for attack. Skinner believes that the internal states are too similar to each other for knowledge of them to allow for useful information.

Chapter 5: States of Consciousness

Video Title: *Hypnosis*
Text Section: **Hypnosis: Hypnotic Induction**
Text Page: **214**

Introduction

Ernest Hilgard believed that hypnosis can induce a state of dissociation—a division of consciousness that permits one part of the mind to operate independently of another part. He argued that there is a "hidden observer" during hypnosis that maintains contact with reality. But social-psychological theories view hypnosis as an ordinary state in which changes are produced by conscious faking or by processes of social influence. Both theories may hold some truth.

Hypnosis is a procedure in which a practitioner suggests changes in the sensations, perceptions, thoughts, feelings, or behavior of the subject. Hypnosis dates back to the seventeenth century and has been used successfully to control pain, break bad habits, recall traumatic past events, and other uses. Hypnosis involves a two-stage process: an *induction*, which guides the subject into a suggestible frame of mind; and a *suggestion*, in which the subject responds to the hypnotist's cues depending on the reason for the hypnosis. Although people usually report that this procedure feels involuntary, in actuality, it is voluntary.

Make a Hypothesis

- Do you think it is hard to induce hypnosis?

  Answer: If hypnosis is a social suggestion, then it would depend upon how likely a person is to follow the particular social suggestion. If it is, as Hilgard contends, an actual dissociation of consciousness, then it would depend on how easy it is for us to make this dissociation. In any case, it would seem to depend more on the person than the hypnotist.

The Video in Perspective

- Does the fact that it does not seem to matter how a person is hypnotically induced support the dissociation or social-cognitive explanation of hypnosis? Why?

  Suggested Answer: It can be used to support either. Since it is the person, it could either be how sensitive they are to the suggestions or how easily they are able to dissociate.

Psychological Detective

- If skill, or even having a person present, does not seem important for hypnosis, then what is more important for hypnosis—the characteristics of the person being hypnotized, or the way hypnosis is performed? What are some important implications of this idea?

  Suggested Answer: It seems that this implies that it is the characteristics of the person that are most important for being hypnotized. This can either suggest that the ability to be hypnotized has to do with internal traits of the person, or with their sensitivity to social suggestions.

Chapter 6: Basic Principles of Learning

Video Title: ***Classical Conditioning***
Text Section: **Classical Conditioning**
Text Page: 235

Introduction

Ivan Pavlov, a Russian physiologist, discovered classical conditioning while studying the digestive system in dogs. While studying the digestive system, Pavlov strapped dogs in a harness, placed different types of food in their mouths, and measured the flow of saliva through a tube surgically inserted in the cheek. He found that the dogs would begin to salivate before the food was actually put in their mouths. Pavlov had discovered a very basic form of learning in which an organism comes to associate one stimulus with another.

The basic classical conditioning procedure involves an unconditioned stimulus (US), an unconditioned response (UR), a neutral stimulus, a conditioned stimulus (CS), and a conditioned response (CR). The salivary reflex is an innate unconditioned response (UR) that is naturally associated by placing food in the mouth, an unconditioned stimulus (US). Pavlov conducted an experiment in which he repeatedly rang a bell before placing food in the dog's mouth. After a series of these paired trials, the dog salivated to the sound of the bell alone. Because the bell, which was initially a neutral stimulus, came to elicit the response through its association with food, it became a conditioned stimulus (CS) and salivation, a conditioned response (CR). Through learning, a previously neutral stimulus evoked the same response as the unconditioned stimulus had.

Make a Hypothesis

- Do you think that a dog can be conditioned to react to a neutral stimulus (a metronome) that has been paired with an unpleasant stimulus, such as electric shock?

  Answer: In the text, you read that the dog can learn to react to a neutral stimulus, like a bell, and to a positive stimulus such as food. In Pavlov's theory, it does not make any difference whether the unconditioned stimulus is positive or negative, so this kind of learning ought to take place.

The Video in Perspective

- What are the US, UR, CS, CR in this example of conditioning?

  Suggested Answer: The US is shock. The UR is a defensive reflex. The CS is the metronome and the CR is a defensive reflex.

Psychological Detective

- Can you think of how this example of classical conditioning may play a role in the development of phobias?

  Suggested Answer: A neutral stimulus paired with a frightening experience could later elicit the fear response.

Video Title:	***Little Albert***
Text Section:	**Classical Conditioning: John Watson, Little Albert and the Ethics of Research**
Text Page:	**239**

Introduction

In John Watson and Rosalie Rayner's 1920 study of "Little Albert," the researchers wanted to determine if emotions can be experimentally conditioned, and if so, whether these learned emotions would transfer, or generalize, to other objects.

The subject was a normal, healthy, 11-month-old infant named "Little Albert." Watson and Rayner attempted to condition the boy to fear a white laboratory rat. Watson presented Albert with a harmless white rat. Then just as Albert reached for the animal, Watson made a loud, crashing sound by banging a steel bar with a hammer behind Albert. The noise frightened the boy and made him cry.

Make a Hypothesis

- Will Little Albert develop a fear response to the rat? What about to a dog or rabbit?

  Answer: This kind of learning is just like what was done to the dog in the Pavlov video on Classical Conditioning. So Little Albert should develop a fear of the rat. Since the dog and rabbit share many characteristics with the rat (fur, four legs, etc.), and since the child is very young and may not make the same sorts of discriminations adults make, the child should generalize the fear response to the dog and the rabbit.

The Video in Perspective

- How is this like classical conditioning? What are the US, UR, CS, CR? In what ways does this study violate ethical research?

  Suggested Answer: The rat is a neutral stimulus paired with a frightening stimulus (the loud sound). The US is the sound, the UR is the startle and frightened response, the CS is the rat, the CR is the fear to the rat. This violates ethics at least in that the experiment generated unnecessary discomfort in the child.

Psychological Detective

- How would you alleviate Little Albert of his fear? Would this work for other fears? Should this study still be discussed even with its ethical problems?

  Suggested Answer: Either use extinction or pair the rat with a positive stimulus and recondition. This latter idea is the basis for systematic desensitization. For the last question the student should be sensitive to both what was learned (the benefits) and the costs (the discomfort to the child).

Video Title: *Operant Conditioning*
Text Section: Operant Conditioning: Shaping
Text Page: 253

Introduction

B.F. Skinner introduced *operant conditioning*, the process by which organisms learn to behave in ways that produce reinforcement. The behavior is "operant" because it operates on the environment to produce reinforcement. Skinner defined reinforcement as any stimulus that increases the likelihood of a prior response. Reinforcers can be either positive or negative, but both result in strengthening a prior response. A positive reinforcer strengthens a prior response through the presentation of a positive stimulus. A negative reinforcer strengthens a response through the removal of an aversive stimulus. Punishment has the opposite effect, decreasing the likelihood of a prior response. There are two types of punishment: positive and negative. A positive punisher weakens a response through the presentation of an aversive stimulus. A negative punisher weakens a response by the removal of a stimulus typically characterized as positive.

But this does not explain how new behavior is acquired. How is a new behavior produced? Skinner proposed *shaping*, a procedure in which reinforcements are used to gradually guide an animal or person toward a specific behavior. A new response is shaped, or guided, by the reinforcement of responses that come closer and closer to the desired behavior.

Make a Hypothesis

- How would you shape a pigeon to bow?

  Answer: Shaping is the reinforcing of successive approximations to a behavior, so you want to start by reinforcing any movement that is like a bow—for example, a small dip of the head. Then, after that behavior is established, make the reinforcement contingent upon dipping the head even further. Continue in this fashion until the whole bow is achieved.

The Video in Perspective

- How is operant conditioning different from classical conditioning? What are some every day examples of shaping?

Suggested Answer: In classical conditioning you are dealing with reflexes (US to UR) for operant conditioning. Voluntary or emitted behavior is what is being conditioned. Here is an everyday example of shaping: education. Each grade, class, test, tries to reinforce more complex educated behavior than what had gone before.

Psychological Detective

- How is shaping similar to getting an animal on a reinforcement schedule? Would it be possible to get an animal to respond so hard for a pellet of food that they actually expended more energy than they ate?

  Suggested Answer: In both shaping and building up to a reinforcement schedule, you build up to the desired response or level or responding. Actually, an animal can be conditioned to respond more for a pellet than it gives back in food using a fixed ratio schedule.

Video Title: *Observational Learning and Human Aggression*
Text Section: **Observational Learning**
Text Page: 267

Introduction

Albert Bandura extended the concept of learning to allow for people to learn from observation. The person being observed is called a model, and the process is sometimes called modeling. The model can be live, or the model can be viewed from a film or tape. A well-known experiment by Bandura and Walters (1963), one of a series of experiments commonly called "the Bobo doll studies," demonstrated the modeling effect for acts of aggression. Children in the experimental group were shown a film of an adult who repeatedly pummeled and struck an inflated doll. Children in the control group did not watch the film. In the second part of the experiment, children in both groups were allowed to play with the same doll shown in the film.

Make a Hypothesis

- How will the behavior of the children who viewed the aggressive model differ from those that did not view the aggressive model?

  Answer: According to Albert Bandura, the adults will serve as models. These models will allow the children to acquire new behaviors. So the children that see the adults beat up the Bobo doll should behave in a similar manner to the adult models and act aggressively towards the doll. The children that did not view these adults should not behave aggressively towards the Bobo doll.

The Video in Perspective

- Children who saw the film struck the doll more often and more vigorously than a control group of children who had not seen the film. According to social learning theory, how is behavior learned beyond reinforcement and punishment? How might the results have been different if the children had seen the model punished (vicarious punishment)?

  Suggested Answer: Social learning theory goes beyond reinforcement and punishment because the adults served as models for behavior. Direct reinforcement is not necessary. The children might have been less aggressive if the adult model had been punished. Seeing the punishment of the models may serve as a vicarious experience of the punishment and serve to inhibit the behavior in a way similar to direct punishment.

Psychological Detective

- What might these results say about the potential effects of television violence? How can modeling affect children's behavior in ways other than aggression?

Suggested Answer: These studies suggest that media violence may increase the probability of violence in children. There are other factors such as the reinforcement for the violence that the characters experience and direct reinforcement or punishment, for example.

Chapter 7: Memory

Video Title: ***Short-Term Memory***
Text Section: **Traditional Models of Memory: The Atkinson-Shiffrin Model: Short-Term Memory**
Text Page: **283**

Introduction

In the Atkinson-Shiffrin Model of memory, short-term memory (STM) retains information only temporarily. It is a limited-capacity memory system involved in the retention of information for brief periods; it is also used for holding information retrieved from long-term memory for temporary use. Back in the 1950s, George Miller described the short-term memory capacity by the phrase "the magical number seven, plus or minus two." He argued that in memory-span tasks, people consistently are able to store seven list items. This limited capacity to store information in short-term memory can be overcome by grouping items to be remembered into larger units, or chunks. A chunk is a meaningful unit of information, and may be composed of smaller units. Since then, some have questioned Miller's magical number, arguing that estimates of STM's capacity have ranged from 2 items to 20. It is agreed, however, that the capacity of STM is small. Increasing the size of these chunks increases our memory capacity.

This video clip shows portions of the administration of the 1937 Stanford-Binet. In this segment, a boy named Drew is answering memory items related to remembering lists of numbers and sentences.

Make a Hypothesis

- What type of memory does Drew rely on to answer items in the Stanford-Binet? Why?

  Answer: Drew is using short-term memory. He is recalling only the items very briefly after they were read and they are only short lists of items. Given the brief time that the items need to be held and how few can be held at a time, this fits exactly what is expected in short-term memory.

The Video in Perspective

- What are the functions of short-term memory? How would it relate to long-term memory?

  Suggested Answer: Short-term memory holds that information needed immediately. It relates to long-term memory in that for us to "remember" something from long-term memory we need to bring it to short-term memory.

Psychological Detective

- How would George Miller explain the ability of Drew to remember sentences with many more words than he could lists of numbers?

  Suggested Answer: Drew is using larger chunks in the words than the numbers.

Chapter 8: Thinking and Intelligence

Video Title: *Experiments on Ape Problem Solving*
Text Section: Thinking: Problem Solving
Text Page: 324

Introduction

There are four basic problem-solving processes: trial and error, algorithms, heuristics, and insight. Trial and error is the simplest strategy, in which several solutions are attempted until one is found that works. An algorithm is a systematic strategy that is guaranteed to produce a solution, but take time. A heuristic is a rule of thumb that works sometimes but does not guarantee a correct outcome. Insight is a form of problem solving in which the solution seems to occur to a person in a sudden moment.

Insight seems to occur whenever people who are stumped with a problem relax the way they approach a problem, reframe it, remove a mental block, or identify an analogy from a prior experience.

Wolfgang Köhler attempted to determine how chimpanzees problem solve; specifically, he studied whether chimpanzees were capable of insight. To answer this question, Köhler put bananas and a long stick outside the chimp's cage, both out of reach, and put a short stick inside the cage with the chimp. Köhler wondered whether the chimp would be able to figure out how to get the bananas.

Make a Hypothesis

- How will the chimp solve the problem? Trial and error? Algorithm? Heuristic? Insight?

  Answer: Trial and error problem solving is characterized by trying several solutions in no organized fashion until the problem is solved. An algorithm is following a precise pattern of steps that will always solve a problem. A heuristic is using a rule of thumb that often works but can sometimes actually make the solution harder. An insight occurs when a brand new solution is reached apparently from using the mind to develop this solution. Chimps are very similar to us in many ways and capable of many of the same behaviors. One of these similarities is very simple tool use. From this, the chimps should use insight to get the bananas.

The Video in Perspective

- Did the chimpanzees show evidence of insight in their problem solving? What behavior did they show that is important to your conclusion?

  Suggested Answer: The behavior seemed purposeful in that the ape directly put the two sticks together without trying other behaviors.

Psychological Detective

- Does this mean that the chimpanzee has consciousness? Is insight just unconscious trial and error or something completely different? Why or why not?

  Suggested Answer: Whatever this means, it means that the chimpanzee is capable of complex mental operations without having to try each idea out in behavior.

Video Title: *Mental Age Testing*
Text Section: Intelligence: The History of Intelligence Testing
Text Page: 341

Introduction

Alfred Binet is known for introducing the idea of intelligence testing. Binet was hired by the Minister of Public Instruction in France to develop an objective way of identifying children who would have difficulty in school. Binet and Theodore Simon developed the first scale for measuring intelligence on skills necessary in an academic setting. Binet and Simon used the test to determine a student's *mental age*, a measure of mental development expressed in terms of the average mental ability at a given age. The Stanford-Binet is an American version of Binet's intelligence test that yields an IQ score with an average of 100.

In this video clip, observe how various types of test items vary from one age level to another. The items in each category will be illustrated by 2-, 5-, and 8-year-old subjects. Note the increasing difficulty of test items with increasing age. This segment illustrates the typical language development items of the Stanford-Binet.

Make a Hypothesis

- What type of language questions do you think will be asked of a 2-year-old? 5-year-old? 8-year-old?

  Answer: In intelligence testing, a person is compared to other people at the same age. Thus, the questions should be much simpler about language for the younger children. The 2-year-old child may simply point to objects that match words that are said because they have not been taught to read. The 8-year-old will have to do more reading because they are in school.

The Video in Perspective

- Why is IQ in this method of measuring not representative of adult intelligence? What factors other than intelligence might influence a child's performance on a test of this type?

  Suggested Answer: An adult's mental age would not keep up with their chronological age. Other factors might include they quality of school and home life, the amount of outside reading done, etc.

Psychological Detective

- Using the Standford-Binet definition of IQ (see page 342 in the text), if a two-year-old child has an MA of 6, what is her IQ? If a five-year-old child has an MA of 5, what is his IQ? If an eight-year-old child has an MA of 6, what is his IQ? Did you think any of the test items shown in the video were biased? If so, how?

  Suggested Answer: The two-year-old would have an IQ of 300, the five-year-old would have an IQ of 100, and the eight-year-old would have an IQ of 75. The case for bias rests in that the items reflect what is taught in our culture. To the extent these questions represent the types of tasks that benefit those that have gone through our schools, they reflect bias.

Video Title: *Capacity to Learn*
Text Section: Intelligence: The History of Intelligence Testing
Text Page: 341

Introduction

Intelligence refers to the capacity to learn from experience and adapt successfully to one's environment. Different theoretical approaches to the study of intelligence contribute to our understanding of intelligence. The psychometric approach to intelligence focuses on how well people do on standardized aptitude tests. In contrast, the cognitive approach focuses on strategies people use in problem-solving.

In 1905, Alfred Binet and Theodore Simon devised the first intelligence test to identify children who were likely to experience difficulty in school and would need special education. Intelligence tests, such as the Stanford-Binet, provide an IQ that represents a person's performance relative to the average of same-age peers. In this video clip, Dr. Inhelder discusses her view of what is measured by a standard intelligence test as compared to what is implicit in Piaget's cognitive developmental theory.

Make a Hypothesis

- How is the Stanford-Binet related to the Piagetian theory of cognitive development?

  Answer: In Piaget's theory, there is a distinction between a person's capacity to learn, their competence, which depends in part on that person's cognitive developmental level, and the person's performance, which is more related to what a person has assimilated or accommodated. Since intelligence tests rest heavily on what has been learned, it would seem to be related to performance and not competence.

The Video in Perspective

- How was the intelligence quotient, or the IQ, originally defined? How is it defined today?

  Suggested Answer: IQ was originally defined as the mental age of the child divided by the chronological age of the child times 100. It is not defined by the performance of the child on the test as compared to others. Commonly given a mean of 100 and standard deviation of 15.

Psychological Detective

- What is the distinction between performance and competence? According to Dr. Inhelder, which is more important to know about a child—performance or competence?

  Suggested Answer: Performance is what a child can do; competence is what a child at that cognitive stage is ultimately capable of doing. This competence is more important because it suggests the actual ultimate ability and not just what is currently in the child's abilities.

Chapter 9: Developmental Psychology I: Conception Through Childhood

Video Title: *Nature and Development of Affection*
Text Section: **Psychosocial Development in Childhood: Attachment**
Text Page: **389**

Introduction

Harry Harlow's 1958 study of the nature of love was a study of the origins of attachment. He was interested specifically in whether infants are drawn to their mothers for the comfort of her warmth and body or for the food she provides. To answer this question, Harlow placed newborn monkeys into a cage that contained two surrogate "mothers"—one was a wire-mesh cylinder, the other was covered with terrycloth. Half were nursed from a bottle in the wire mother's body and half from the cloth mother.

Make a Hypothesis

- Do you think that the newborn monkeys will prefer the cloth "mother" or the wire "mother"?

Answer: Freud developed the concept that attachment was based on food as an explanation for why children attach to mothers. Harlow developed the concept that attachment is based on contact comfort. Since, the cloth mother is much more pleasant to be near, the monkey should attach to the cloth "mother."

The Video in Perspective

- The newborn monkeys spent almost all of their time with the terrycloth surrogate mother. The wire mother was identical to the cloth mother in all respects except for the ability to provide "contact comfort." Newborn monkeys showed a clear preference for "contact comfort" over food, regardless of the feeding situation. What was the primary variable determining affection for the mother?

  Suggested Answer: The primary variable was the comfort gained, not the food obtained from the mother.

Psychological Detective

- How might this work be compared to the work on attachment done by Mary Ainsworth? How important is this first relationship?

  Suggested Answer: In Ainsworth, the study was about the quality of attachment. Even though the monkey was attached, there is a question about the quality of the attachment to this very nonresponsive mother. These studies suggest that that the first attachments are very important to the child or they would not use them as a base for exploration.

Video Title:	***Sensorimotor Development***
Text Section:	**Cognitive Development in Childhood: Piaget's Theory: The Sensorimotor Stage**
Text Page:	**399**

Introduction

Jean Piaget is the most influential figure in the study of cognitive development. Piaget's theory is based on the premise that children are active, constructive thinkers who want to understand their world. Children learn about the world around them by forming *schemas*, mental representations of the world which guide the processes of assimilation and accommodation. Further, children progress through a series of cognitive stages, each characterized by a specific kind of thinking: sensorimotor, preoperational, concrete operational, and formal operational.

The first stage, the sensorimotor stage, begins at birth and lasts about two years. Infants learn about their world through direct sensory and motor contact, such as touching, sucking, and manipulating objects. The major achievement during this stage is *object permanence*, the understanding that an object continues to exist even when you can't see it or touch it. Separation anxiety also develops during this stage.

Make a Hypothesis

- What do you think will be some of the important cognitive developments during the sensorimotor stage?

  Answer: According to Piaget, the child at birth conceives of the world as being that which is present to the child's senses at any moment. Thus, an important cognitive development in the first two years is to be able to realize that objects exist independently of the child and thus exist even though the child does not see or hear them. This will allow the child ultimately to think with symbols (such as language) and to think abstractly.

The Video in Perspective

- According to Piaget, mental functioning depends on what two inborn processes? What major accomplishments characterize each stage of cognitive development?

Suggested Answer: The two processes are accommodation and assimilation. The accomplishments are below. Note this is phrased as accomplishments, not lacks, so some accomplishments are in a stage earlier than usual because the lack is remedied before the child can move on to the next stage.

Stage	Major Accomplishment
Sensorimotor	*Object Permanence and/or symbolic functions*
Preoperational	*Conservation*
Concrete Operations	*Beginning of abstract thinking*
Formal Operations	*Abstract thinking*

Psychological Detective

• Why does Piaget believe that cognitive development begins before language? Does his description of the sensorimotor stage indicate that cognitive development is in stages or is gradual? Why?

Suggested Answer: Cognitive development begins before language for Piaget at least in part because of the development of the object concept. If the student argues for a gradual development, the student needs to focus on all the small steps described by Piaget. If the student wants to argue for stages, then the student needs to focus on the similarity of the mental activity at all parts of this first stage.

Video Title: ***Teaching Sign Language to the Chimpanzee Washoe***
Text Section: **Language: Language Development**
Text Page: **403**

Introduction

Some comparative psychologists argue that animals have the capacity to acquire language and have attempted to demonstrate that the language barrier between humans and animals can be broken.

In 1966, a chimpanzee named Washoe came to the laboratory of Allen and Beatrice Gardner at the University of Nevada. The Gardners raised Washoe with constant human companionship and provided many social interactions. Because American Sign Language (ASL) doesn't require speech and the chimpanzee's hand is similar to the human hand, ASL was the chosen technique for teaching language to Washoe. Sign language was integrated into Washoe's daily life. Spoken words were never used in Washoe's presence. The researchers wanted to learn if a chimpanzee was capable of acquiring language.

Make a Hypothesis

• Do you think that Washoe will be able to communicate using ASL?

Answer: Chimpanzees are our closest relatives in the animal kingdom. They share many abilities, including insight (see the video on Animal Intelligence). They form social groups and communicate in complex ways in the wild. However, they lack the ability to make speech sound. But they do have the ability to make many sophisticated motions with their fingers. So they ought to be able to do some communication using ASL, but it should be more simple than what humans can do.

The Video in Perspective

• Does the language seem like that of a child's or adult's?

Suggested Answer: This language level is simple even by children's standards.

Psychological Detective

- Allen and Beatrice Gardner (1969) taught American Sign Language (ASL) to Washoe. Within 4 years, Washoe had a vocabulary of 132 words and could combine signs to form simple sentences. Washoe also communicated in sign language to other chimps and taught her adopted son 68 different signs. Does Washoe show the properties of important characteristics such as syntax in her "language" behavior?

  Suggested Answer: Syntax is often lacking, particularly word order.

Chapter 10: Developmental Psychology II: Adolescence Through Old Age

Video Title: *Fluid & Crystallized Intelligence*
Text Section: Intellectual Changes: Early Intelligence: Types of Intelligence
Text Page: 421

Introduction

Psychologists used to believe that intelligence peaks in the early twenties, declines gradually up to the age of fifty, then drops dramatically from that point on. We now know that old age does not necessarily diminish intelligence. It is now known that there are two general intelligence factors, not just one.

In this video clip, Raymond Cattell distinguishes between fluid and crystallized intelligence. Fluid intelligence refers to the capacity for deductive reasoning and the ability to use new information to solve problems. Examples of this type of intelligence include rote memory and spatial and visual imagery skills. Crystallized intelligence reflects the accumulation of verbal skills and factual knowledge. This type of intelligence includes verbal and numerical skills. Fluid intelligence is independent of education and experience, whereas crystallized intelligence depends on culture, education, and experience.

Make a Hypothesis

- Do you think that traditional intelligence tests, like the Stanford-Binet, are more a measure of fluid or crystallized intelligence?

  Answer: Most intelligence tests requires our ability to extract information from long-term memory and to use a lot of well practiced skills. Thus intelligence tests primarily measure crystallized intelligence.

The Video in Perspective

- What developmental changes are related to the fluid/crystallized distinction? Which do you think will decline faster as we age?

  Suggested Answer: Fluid intelligence declines more with age than does crystallized intelligence.

Psychololgical Detective

- What are some personal examples of fluid intelligence and crystallized intelligence for you? Why is the distinction between fluid and crystallized intelligence important?

  Suggested Answer: Examples of fluid intelligence would be learning new skills and applying knowledge to new situations. These tasks would include what students are doing in classes. An example of crystallized intelligence would be the SAT. The distinction is that the fluid abilities help them in getting new skills while crystallized skills let them rely on previously learned skills so that they can work harder to learn the new skills.

Video Title:	*Intimacy versus Isolation*
Text Section:	**Personality and Social Change: Early Adulthood: Intimacy Versus Isolation**
Text Page	**421**

Introduction

Erik Erikson proposed a psychosocial theory of development. According to Erikson's life-span approach, people progress through eight stages from infancy through adulthood, each marked by a psychosocial crisis that has to be resolved.

During the first stage, in infancy, the primary crisis is called *trust versus mistrust*. During the second stage, toddlers experience *autonomy versus shame and doubt*. In the third stage, the primary crisis for preschoolers is *initiative versus guilt*. During the elementary school years, the primary crisis involves *industry versus inferiority*. For adolescents, the fifth stage involves *identity versus role confusion*. Adolescents struggle to break from parents and form an identity, or self-concept. During the sixth stage, the young adult, having resolved the identity crisis, seeks intimacy in meaningful close relationships and marriage. The primary crisis during young adulthood is *intimacy versus isolation*. Middle adulthood is marked by *generativity versus stagnation*. Middle-age adults seeks to contribute to a new generation at work, at home, and in the community. In the final stage, *integrity versus despair*, older adults seek integrity, a sense that their lives were worthwhile.

Make a Hypothesis

- What do you think Erikson means by "intimacy"?

  Answer: Since the goal of adolescence has been to form an identity and the ultimate goal of this theory to see your place in the world, it seems that intimacy is to connect very strongly with at least one other person. Here you are going beyond yourself, even giving up some of that identity for the sake of being with another person.

The Video in Perspective

- According to Erikson, will a person be able to form true intimacy if they have not yet solved the psychosocial issue of developing an identity? Why?

  Suggested Answer: No, a person will not form true intimacy without developing an identity. Intimacy requires fusing an identity with that of another and so is impossible to have without an identity.

Psychological Detective

- How might cultural and social factors influence the psychosocial development in Erikson's theory, in general, and of intimacy, in particular?

  Suggested Answer: The stages were developed to match the developmental patterns of the West. Other cultures may time the events of life differently so the crises will occur at different times of life. Intimacy may be directly relevant here because with different cultures the ages that people get married varies a great deal.

Chapter 12: Personality

Video Title: *The Unconscious*
Text Section: The Psychodynamic Perspective: Freud in Perspective: The Neo-Freudians
Text Page: 518

Introduction

Psychodynamic theories explain behavior and personality in terms of unconscious energy dynamics within the individual. Carl Jung was a neo-Freudian theorist who agreed with Freud that human behavior is influenced by the unconscious, but he disagreed with Freud on two points in particular. First, there exists not only a personal unconscious but also a *collective unconscious*, the universal memories and experiences of humankind, represented in the unconscious images and symbols of all people. Because of this evolutionary history, certain common themes appear in cultural myths and legends throughout the world. Jung coined the term *archetypes* to refer to these universal, symbolic images that appear in myths, art, dreams, and other expressions of the collective unconscious. Second, Jung argued that people strive for more than just the satisfaction of biological drives. People are motivated not only by the past, but also, future goals and the desire for self-fulfillment.

Make a Hypothesis

- How do you think Carl Jung's meaning of the unconscious differs from Sigmund Freud's?

  Answer: Jung does not see the unconscious as a battleground of three opposing forces as does Freud. It is merely those actions that occur of which we have no knowledge.

The Video in Perspective

- How does Jung argue that we can find out about the unconscious?

  Suggested Answer: We infer the actions of the unconscious because we see behaviors on the part of other people for which they have no knowledge.

Psychological Detective

- What are some other concepts that have been discussed in the course that seem to relate to the concept of the unconscious? What would Skinner think of the concept of the unconscious?

  Suggested Answer: Some examples from earlier chapters of the book include: basic sensations, dreams, some memory phenomena including the repressed memories, the sensorimotor child. Skinner would not make a distinction between conscious and unconscious and would see no more utility in that concept than he would emotions or achievement motivation.

Chapter 13: Psychological Disorders

Video Title: *The Three Faces of Eve*
Text Section: **Anxiety, Somatoform, and Dissociative Disorder: Dissociative Disorders: Dissociative Identity Disorder**
Text Page: **551**

Introduction

The DSM-IV defines dissociative disorders as conditions in which consciousness or identity is split or altered. This category includes amnesia, fugue, and dissociative identity disorder.

Dissociative identity disorder is a controversial disorder marked by the appearance within one person of two or more distinct personalities, each with its own name and traits; it is also called multiple personality disorder.

In *The Three Faces of Eve*, a woman alternates among Eve White, Eve Black, and Jane. Eve White is conventional, modest and unassuming, moralistic, and enveloped in sadness. Eve Black is self-centered, deceitful, and focused on immediate pleasures. Jane is a balance of the two Eves. She has an awareness of what both Eves do.

Make a Hypothesis

- What do you think are common symptoms of dissociative identity disorder?

  Answer: From the name given to the disorder, the person is to have distinct identities. These identities should differ in characteristics of behavior, mannerisms, and even names. These identities should take turns being present.

The Video in Perspective

- What are the possible explanations for dissociative identity disorder? How is this debate like the debate over hypnosis?

  Suggested Answer: The two main positions are the same as for hypnosis: the personalities are responses to social suggestion or the result of dissociation. Some of the same people are involved.

Psychological Detective

- After reading the text's description of the controversy and viewing the videotape of Eve, do you believe that Eve had three actually distinct personalities? What would it take to conclusively demonstrate that a person has more than one personality?

  Suggested Answer: The student should look for evidence of real changes in traits and behaviors.

Chapter 14: Therapy

Video Title: *The Role of the Therapist*
Text Section: **Psychologically Based Therapies: Humanistic Therapies: Client-Centered Therapy**
Text Page: **590**

Introduction

Humanist therapies assume that people seek self-actualization and self-fulfillment. It was Carl Rogers who redefined the role of a therapist to be that of facilitator for the client. Rogers' approach has been called client-centered, person-centered, and nondirective. According to Rogers, if certain conditions are present in the therapist, then change will occur in the client. Rogers' theory is based on the tendency toward self-actualization, the need to fulfill one's unique potential.

Make a Hypothesis

- What conditions do you think are important to the counselor relationship in client-centered therapy?

  Answer: For Carl Rogers, mental disorders are largely the result of being inauthentic. In order to heal, the person needs to develop an authentic or true view of their self. To see how this works, the counselor must be authentic as well.

The Video in Perspective

- What are the three conditions necessary for successful therapy according to Rogers? Which is the most important? Why?

  Suggested Answer: The three conditions are the genuineness of the therapist as a person, the ability of the therapist to accept the client as a person without judgment (unconditional positive regard), and empathy. The most important is the genuineness of the therapist. It is most important because that is the goal of therapy for the client to become genuine and so the therapist must model that behavior.

Psychological Detective

- How is client-centered therapy similar to other humanistic therapies? How is it similar and different from psychodynamic therapies?

  Suggested Answer: Client-centered therapy is similar to other humanistic in its concern for growth. Client-centered therapy is similar to psychodynamic therapies in that both seek for the client to have a greater understanding of who they are. Client-centered therapy, however, sees the goal for the person to become more genuinely who they are, and psychodynamic therapies don't necessarily see that as the goal.

Chapter 15: Health Psychology

Video Title: *Self-Actualization*
Text Section: Coping with Stress: Psychological Moderators of Stress
Text Page: 657

Introduction

Most health psychologists contend that certain personality traits are healthier and more adaptive than others. Hardiness, optimism, and hope have all been identified as traits that contribute to a "self-healing personality." For instance, Suzanne Kobasa studied 200 business executives under stress and found a link between stress and illness. She identified *hardiness* as a personality trait that acted as a buffer against stress.

Another example of the importance of the self-healing personality can be seen in Carl Rogers' personality theory. According to Rogers, the needs for self-actualization and positive regard present a potential for conflict. That is, unconditional positive regard permits self-actualization, but conditioned positive regard can result in self-discrepancies. Further, when Rogers evaluated the importance of the self-concept, he found that as clients progressed in therapy and made more and more positive statements about themselves, self-discrepancies diminished.

Make a Hypothesis

- What is the source of maladjustment, and by extension to a personality that could damage health, according to Rogers?

  Answer: The person strives to their ideal self in Rogers' theory. However, if their view of their self is not accurate, then they will not fulfill the needs of their true self in any meaningful way. This is Rogers' definition of maladjustment.

The Video in Perspective

- What are other personality features that might mediate health and our response to stress?

  Suggested Answer: The book discusses hardiness, explanatory style, and even a sense of humor as personality factors involved in health.

Psychological Detective

- What is self-actualization? How might it act as a psychological mediator in health?

  Suggested Answer: Self-actualization, according to Rogers, is when the perceived self is in accord with who we really are and so it can change and grow along with the organism (the actual self). It is a mediator of health because when our perceived self is not growing it leads to maladjustment and damaging behaviors.

Chapter 16: Social Psychology: The Individual in Society

Video Title: *Bystander Apathy*
Text Section: Interpersonal Relations: Prosocial Behavior: Helping Others: Situational and Personal Influences on Helping Behaviors
Text Page: 688

Introduction

The murder of Kitty Genovese in New York City in March of 1964 was a sort of wake-up call to social psychology and the impetus for studying *bystander effect*. Kitty Genovese was returning to her apartment in a middle-class neighborhood when a man attacked her with a knife. The stabbing lasted 35 minutes. What was most surprising was that 38 people witnessed the attack, but only one had called the police. If someone would have helped sooner, she may not have died.

Social psychologists Bibb Latané and John Darley studied the social factors at work in this situation of *bystander apathy*. In a series of social psychological experiments, they staged emergencies, varied the conditions, and observed what took place. In one such study, psychology students were invited to participate in an interview supposedly to discuss urban university life. When they arrived for the interview, a secretary told them to go to a room and fill out a questionnaire. Subjects filled out questionnaires alone or in groups of three. After being seated for a few minutes, white smoke was pumped into the room from a vent, filling the room with smoke. Subjects were timed to see how long before they would go and get some help.

Make a Hypothesis

- Do you think people will be less likely to make an emergency interpretation of an event if they are in the presence of other people or if they are alone?

  Answer: When others are around, we use them to determine if the emergency is real or not, or expect someone else to have taken care of the problem. So when we are in a group, we are less likely to respond to the emergency than when we are alone.

The Video in Perspective

- Latané and Darley found that 55 percent of the subjects in the alone condition reported the smoke within the first two minutes, whereas 12 percent of the subjects who were in the presence of others did so. What accounts for the differences in the two conditions? What factors inhibit a response to an emergency?

  Suggested Answer: The independent variable—i.e., the presence of other people— accounts for the difference in the responses of the two groups. The factors behind this difference in the response rate could be diffusion of responsibility, ambiguity of the situation, the use of others as guides to the nature of a situation, etc.

Psychological Detective

- How might the *bystander effect* play a role in the murder of Kitty Genovese? How can bystander intervention in emergencies be increased?

  Suggested Answer: Here the fact that others could have seen the situation played the inhibitory role in the responses of the bystanders. To increase bystander intervention, emergencies need to be clear, and the responsibility of each person needs to be identified.

Video Title: *Obedience*
Text Section: Social Influences on Behavior: Obedience
Text Page: 700

Introduction

In 1963, Stanley Milgram, partly as an attempt to understand the Holocaust, conducted an experiment to determine people's willingness to obey authority figures, even if it meant harming another person in doing so.

The subjects were 40 males. Each subject was paid to participate in the study at Yale University. The subject was seated next to another "subject" who was actually a confederate. The subjects were told that the study was on the effects of punishment on learning. There was a drawing to determine who would be the "teacher" and who would be the "learner" in the experiment, but actually, the drawing was rigged so that the subjects were always the teacher and the confederate was always the learner. The subject watched as the learner was then strapped to a chair and hooked up to electrodes connected to a shock generator. The learner is told that he is to learn a list of word pairs and that every time he makes an error, he will receive electric shocks of increasing levels.

The teacher is then taken to an adjoining room and seated in front of the shock generator ranging from 15 volts to 450 volts (SLIGHT SHOCK to DANGER: SEVERE SHOCK), in increments of 15 volts. The experimenter instructed the teacher to give an electric shock each time the learner responded incorrectly. He was to start with 15 volts and to increase the level of shock each time the learner made an error. Obedience was measured by recording the level of shock at which each subject refused to continue administering shock.

Make a Hypothesis

- What percentage of subjects do you predict delivered shock all the way up to 450 volts—"DANGER: SEVERE SHOCK"?

  Answer: Milgram surveyed clinical psychologists of his day describing his experiment and asking this question. In his survey he found that the clinical psychologists expected only severely mentally ill persons of certain types to go all the way. So Milgram expected few to go all the way to the 450 volts level.

However, we know from studies like Solomon Asch's that there are powerful forces that lead us to conform, especially to those in authority. So a substantial percentage should go all the way to the end of the shock levels.

The Video in Perspective

- Sixty-five percent of the subjects followed the experimenter's orders and delivered the highest level of shock to the learner. What would *you* have done if you were a subject in this experiment? Why? What factors in this situation contributed to such a high degree of obedience? Suppose you are on a research panel to approve or reject Milgram's study of obedience today. Would you approve or reject his study? On what ethical guidelines do you base your answer?

  Suggested Answer: Students tend to think they will be in the minority. They need to see that those that went on were not that different from them. The factor that led to the obedience was the presence of an authority figure that took responsibility for the actions. The approval or disapproval of the study needs to rest on the importance of the finding (when done and what was known then is important) and the harm done to the subjects and the impact of the deception both on the subjects and the image of psychology.

Psychological Detective

- Can you cite examples of how people have complied with authority at any cost in our society's history? Why do you think people obey orders from authority figures? Are there ways to reduce such blind obedience to authorities?

  Suggested Answer: Examples are the holocaust and many other war crimes where solders said they were following orders. Other examples include unethical behavior in a work situation where employees claim to be doing only what the boss told them to do. Reasons for the high level of obedience could be that it is well reinforced, needed for the smooth functioning of society, needed for social approval from powerful figures, etc. Ways to reduce such blind obedience might include making the rules such that the lower level person in an action still have responsibility for their actions.

Chapter 17: Industrial and Organizational Psychology

Video Title: *Personality Traits*
Text Section: Personnel Psychology: Using Personality Tests in Selecting Police Officers
Text Page: 721

Introduction

Gordon Allport was a leading personality theorist. He argued that the study of personality must begin with description and measurement. Allport described personality by using *traits*, a descriptive characteristic of an individual, assumed to be stable across situations and time. Allport noted that most people in a society share common traits that are expected and rewarded by their culture. To understand differences in personality, Allport studied individual characteristics that make each person unique.

Another major trait theorist was Raymond Cattell, who used factor analysis to identify clusters of traits. This procedure identifies clusters of correlated items that seem to be measuring the same underlying trait, ability, or aptitude. Cattell found sixteen source traits to sufficiently describe personality. Cattell developed the Sixteen Personality Factors Questionnaire (16 PF), a 187-item scale that yields sixteen separate scores, one for each factor. From Cattell's factor analysis and other trait models, five factors have emerged from various personality questionnaires. This is sometimes called the Big 5 personality factors.

Although not all researchers adhere to this model, evidence in support of this five-factor model is widespread. These traits can be measured by personality inventories. One of the most important contributions of trait psychology is the construction of personality inventories—questionnaires designed to assess a whole multitude of traits. The use of these inventories has been of increasing interest to industrial and organizational psychologists in many ways. In this video clip, Allport distinguishes between cardinal and central traits.

Introduction

- How do you think Gordon Allport distinguishes between cardinal traits and central traits? And how might they relate to personality inventories such as the Big 5 personality inventory?

  Answer: The difference between cardinal and central traits is on a continuum. A cardinal trait is a trait that some people have that is visible in all that person's behaviors. Central traits are those that are most characteristic in a person, but no one trait is seen in every behavior. Finally, the Big 5 would probably be considered central traits. These traits are thought to be a small collection of traits that are characteristic of most people and cover most situations.

The Video in Perspective

- According to Gordon Allport, is it sufficient to know what traits a person has? How could simply looking at a list of traits of a person lead to an incorrect conclusion?

  Suggested Answer: According to Allport, it is not sufficient to know what traits a person has. You need to know what role those traits play in a person. A cardinal trait will overwhelm all others. Central traits are more important than others. Without knowing the role a trait plays, you might not accurately understand a person's behavior.

Psychological Detective

- Does Allport's theory suggest it is a good idea or a poor idea to use inventories to select personnel such as police officers?

  Suggested Answer: Unless you know the role that trait plays in a person, such use of inventories will be risky at best. A person with a central trait of aggressiveness will behave very differently than a person who has that trait as a secondary trait.